3/97

Style
Ch'uan

-six Movements

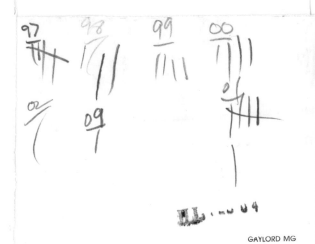

Chinese Martial Arts Series 3

Chen Style T'ai Chi Ch'uan

Thirty-six and Fifty-six Movements

by Xing Yanling

Translated by Mei Xuexiong

SUGAWARA MARTIAL ARTS INSTITUTE / JAPAN PUBLICATIONS

Chinese Martial Arts Series 3
Chen Style T'ai Chi Ch'uan
—Thirty-six and Fifty-six Movements
Written and Performed by Xing Yanling (Shing Yenling)
Under the technical supervision of Professor Wang Peikun
Translated by Mei Xuexiong (Mei Sueshiong)
Proofread by Osborne Denise
Edited by Tetsutaka Sugawara and Xing Yanling

Published by
Sugawara Martial Arts Institute Inc.
20-13, Tadao 3 chome, Machida-shi, Tokyo, 194 Japan
Phone: 0427-94-0972 / FAX: 0427-94-0899

First printing: March 1993
Second printing: August 1996

ISBN: 0-87040-909-3
Printed in Japan

Distributors:
UNITED STATES: Kodansha America, Inc., through Farrar, Straus
& Giroux, 19 Union SquareWest, New York, NY 10003.
CANADA: Fitzhenry & Whiteside Ltd., 195 Allstate Parkway,
Markham, Ontario L3R 4T8. UNITED KINGDOM AND
EUROPE: Premier Book Marketing Ltd., 1 Gower Street, London
WC1E 6HA. AUSTRALIA AND NEW ZEALAND: Bookwise
International, 54 Crittenden Road, Findon, South Australia 5023.
THE FAR EAST AND JAPAN: Japan Publications Trading Co.,
Ltd., 1-2-1, Sarugaku-cho, Chiyoda-ku, Tokyo 101.

Contents

Introduction

1. A Brief Introduction to Chen Style Taijiquan

From its origination around the sixties of the seventeenth century up to now, the Chen Style Taijiquan has gone through a history of more than 300 years. As the oldest one among taijiquan schools, it was created by the famous martial arts master Chen Wangting, a native of Chenjiagou, Wen County, Henan Province, China. Although some other popular taijiquan schools such as Yang, Wu and Sun styles have been developed on the base of Chen Style Taijiquan, it has always preserved its original features through the ages. The differences between Chen Style Taijiquan and the other schools include the following.

1) There are prompt and explosive actions embodied in the slow and gentle movements of Chen Style Taijiquan.

2) Chen Style Taijiquan places emphasis on the twining, twisting and spiraling motion which can lead to a strong, changeable and unpredictable offensive or defensive.

3) There are relative difficult movements such as soft neutralization, explosive strike and various jumps in routines of Chen Style.

Chen Style Taijiquan can be divided into several kinds such as Old Form, New Form, Big Frame and Small Frame, and they have their own distinguishing features and multitudinous bare-handed or armed routines. Yet "Chen Style Simplified Taijiquan" and "Competition Routine of Chen Style Taijiquan" introduced in this book were established not long before.

Chen Style Simplified Taijiquan was composed by Kan Guixiang and Tian Xiuchen, teachers at Beijing Institute of Physical Education, on the base of Routine 1 of the Old Form of Chen Style Taijiquan to cater to the need of beginners. The routine of 36 forms simplified from the initial 83 forms is a good introduction for beginners, not only being simple and easy to learn, but also retaining the original characteristics and a fairly high degree

of difficulty.

Competition Routine of Chen Style Taijiquan was brought into being by the Chinese Institute of Martial Arts in 1989 when a group of experts in taijiquan were assembled to compose and verify compulsory competition routines including the traditional sets of Chen, Yang, Wu and Sun Styles and Taiji-swordplay, so that athletes can compete under the same conditions. The demands set by the organizers include three main points. First, the style, the features and the technical essentials of the traditional routines should be preserved; second, the routines should be composed in accordance with modern sports science, especially human physiology, so that they can help to promote the all-round development of people in both mind and body; and third, the routines should possess a fairly high degree of difficulty and conform to competition rules, impelling people to enhance the technical level constantly. Assimilating predecessors' technical skill as well as suiting the needs of contemporary sports, the competition routine of Chen Style Taijiquan therefore turned out to be a typical one with many favourable features. Because of its degree of difficulty and strength requirement, it is precisely considered as a set more suitable for practitioners who have laid a fairly solid foundation of martial arts and want to improve themselves in practice.

2. Characteristics of Chen Style Taijiquan

Chen Style Taijiquan shares the common features that the other schools of taijiquan have. To grasp these common features, you might read Chinese Martial Arts Series 1 (The Basic Exercises) for reference. In short, taijiquan is one of the main branches of Chinese Martial Arts. Its outstanding features are usually described as "having both form and spirit", "combining inside and outside into one". The movements should not only have the form of attack and defence, but also be performed in the spirit of attack and defence. Moreover, all the movements should be in harmony with one's breathing and consciousness, so that the unity of internal spirit and external appearance can be achieved. Like the other schools of martial arts do, movements of taijiquan also consists of skills of kicking, striking, throwing and joint-locking, yet the routine of Yang, Wu and Sun Styles should performed slowly and gently. However, the unique style of Chen Style Taijiquan should not be ignored.

1) Abdominal Paradoxical Respiration

Abdominal paradoxical respiration is contrary to normal method but is specially required in practising Chen Style Taijiquan. The way to carry out this unique breathing is to: Inhale with the lower part of the abdomen gradually pulled in and the chest expanded, and exhale with the lower part of the abdomen slowly bulged out and the chest contracted. In this way, you can strengthen your diaphragm and abdominal muscles, and improve the blood circulation with a broader range of fluctuation of abdominal pressure. Often, the movements of distinct collection or explosive discharge of strength emerge in routines of Chen Style Taijiquan, and the rhythm of motion changes frequently. Thereby, the way of breathing is not immutable and the abdominal paradoxical respiration is not always required. While conducting ordinary movements, you might breathe deeply and naturally, coordinating respiration with actions of the limbs and trunk. However, the moment you are accumulating or exerting strength, speeding up or slowing down the pace to a great extent, the abdominal paradoxical respiration

would make its appearance clearly.

2) Spiral Thread-twining Strength

The thread-twining strength is one of the important features of taijiquan, and it is particularly noticeable with Chen Style. In practising Chen Style Taijiquan, you are required to move your limbs always along circular paths, to apply strength as if twining silk thread or reeling it off a cocoon. The mind is dominant, guiding all actions and directing strength through the joints in proper order. Every section of the body is linked up, so nothing would remain still if any part of the body is in motion. In a sense, taijiquan actually takes the shapes of a ball, with the ankles and the legs , the wrists and the arms, the waist and the spine constantly twisting, therefore manifesting a unique style of uninterrupted spiral motion.

Only in this way can you smoothly neutralize the oncoming force from your opponent while doing push-hand exercises. It can also help you to increase the initial length of the muscles so as accumulate inner power, therefore in discharge, the limbs can be extended explosively like a spring.

3) Strength from Waist and Crotch

Chen Style Taijiquan distinguishes itself from others by its obvious and speedy discharge of strength, one method of which is usually called "strength from waist and crotch". It is actually a combined energy, with the waist as the dominant factor, accompanied by the twist at the hips and the opening-closing motion of the crotch. As the proverb runs, "Waist is the dominator." The centre of the waist is the spine which should remain straight and erect, and it plays an important role in controlling the tension and the relaxation of the lumbar and abdominal muscles and the rotation of the torso. Almost any strength whether it is the internal implicit force or the external exerted power, comes out from the waist and crotch, passes through the limbs and reaches the special part of the body, thus accomplishing a complete discharge of strength.

4) Shaking Power

The shaking power is a combination of the thread-twining strength and the strength from waist and crotch. When the thread-twining strength and the strength from waist and crotch reach the special part of the body that is going to put forth force, they combine into explosive power, causing the part of the body to shake all of a sudden. For instance, while punching, the strength comes out from the waist and crotch, flows through the arm by means of twisting and twining, and reaches the fist as it promptly and spirally strikes at the destination. Just at the moment, with the torso twisting swiftly and the wrist shaking vigorously, the fist springs, exerting a kind of short, strong bouncy power. It is all the same with other parts of the body.

5) Stamp

One of the differences between Chen Style and the other schools is that there are a lot of stamps in routines of Chen Style Taijiquan. Stand on one leg with the other foot raised. As you bend the leg at the knee to squat down, the other foot falls and then forcibly stamps on the floor with a smack. This is called "single stamp". On landing after a jump, both feet stamp on the floor in quick succession. And this is called "double stamps". A stamp should be short and firm, and usually be accompanied by abdominal paradoxical respiration. Inhale with the abdomen pulled in when the front rises; direct the energy stream down while the foot falls; and exhale when the whole sole of the foot strongly and promptly stamps on the

floor. A sound can also be given with the expiration and notice must be taken to lower the hips and release force when the foot touches the ground.

6) Hardness and Softness Supplementing Each Other, Quickness Alternating with Slowness

During the process of doing Chen Style Taijiquan, the changes from hardness to softness, from quickness to slowness are particularly noticeable. The moving or transitive phase of an action stresses softness, while the phase when a special part of the body reaches a final position places emphasis on hardness. Generally speaking, softness means a slow pace of movement and continuous twining. However, hardness can be divided into three circumstances. First, you can only slightly speed up the motion, applying inner power; second, you should accelerate the action to exert strength; and third, you should quicken the movement sharply, utilizing explosively power. No matter what it is, the transition from one state to another should be smooth and natural. When it stresses softness, be sure not to be feeble, you ought to guide your energy stream to retain certain force. On the other hand, when it stresses hardness, keep your movements from being stiff and clumsy. You might direct your energy stream to promote your power and apply the strength from the waist and crotch to manifest sturdiness and vigor.

3. Basic Rules of Chen Style Taijiquan

1) Basic Body Positions

While practising taijiquan, you should be calm, getting rid of any distracting thought and concentrating your attention on the exercise. The body should be erect, and the muscles and joints should be naturally relaxed, so that the viscera can be in a comfortable state. The basic requirements for the body are as follows.

A) The Head

In practising taijiquan, the position of the head must be strictly maintained. You should hold the head upright with the neck naturally relaxed and the chin slightly tucked in, as if you were carrying a pitcher of water on the head. The movement of the neck must coordinate with the change in position of the body and the turning of the torso. Be sure not to allow the head to sway. There is a saying relating to this respect: "Leading propping-force up imaginarily". This indicates that you must get a sense of imaginarily pushing the acupuncture point "Baihui" on the top of your head upward, as if your head were hoisted up with a rope. An upright head makes it possible to assume an erect body posture, to preserve a tranquil mind and to keep a vigorous spirit.

The facial expression should be earnest, relaxed and natural. Close the mouth gently with the tongue flat and its tip softly touching the palate. Breathe naturally through the nose. But while you are exerting strength, you can slightly open the mouth so as to promote your power with the expiration through both the nose and the mouth.

B) The Shoulders and the Arms

While in practice, you must see that your shoulders are even, relaxed and lowered. Do not shrug them at any time. Keep the elbows slightly bent and dropped. As a jargon says: "Elbow never clings to ribs, nor does it go far away from ribs." This description means that when you withdraw the arm, you must not bend the elbow excessively and draw it so close as to nestle against the torso, and a space of a standing fist should be left under the armpit so that the arm can move round freely; and while you extend the arm, you must not straighten the elbow completely so that the elbow never goes too far away thereby losing its function to protect the ribs. In fact, the arms should be well rounded throughout the whole process. Be sure to avoid any straight or angled movement.

The wrists should be flexible, moving nimbly and tenaciously in line with the torso and the arms. Much attention should be paid to the subtle changes of the hands which are brought along by the rotation of the arms. The wrist should be sunk in some fixed position such as pushing hand.

C) The Chest and the Back

One of the basic rules is "keeping chest in and back extended". It reminds us that while doing taijiquan, do not throw the chest out, nor draw it too far in, but just keep it slightly restrained. This description also means that the back should be straight so that you can get a sense of "back up". In fact, the muscles on both the chest and the back should be relaxed so as to eliminate tension on the ribs, to guarantee smooth and natural breathing, and to allow the arms to move freely. Be sure not to hump the back.

D) The Spine and the Waist

The spine is the mainstay of human body, playing a most important role in practising taijiquan. It must be held normally erect. You must not arch or jut out any section of it, nor incline it to either side so as to avoid unnecessary muscular tension on the torso. Likewise, the waist, namely the lumbar section of the body, is the central link, harmonizing actions, regulating postures, keeping balance, ensuring freedom of the torso in turning, smoothing the transition of movements from one to another and propelling strength to special part of the body. This is exactly what the saying "waist is

13

the dominator" implies. While in practice, the waist should be naturally relaxed. Do not thrust the belly out, nor draw it too far in. Pull the abdomen slightly in while inhaling, and bulge it slightly out by guiding the energy stream down to the acupuncture point "Dantian" while exhaling. The role of waist is particularly conspicuous in Chen Style Taijiquan. The strength accumulation is fulfilled through obvious twisting at the waist which brings the arm to move. On the other hand, only with swift twisting at the waist can the powerful exertion of strength be accomplished.

E) The Buttocks

Hold the buttocks slightly in and avoid specially protruding them out or tucking them too far in, so as not to spoil the normal position of the body and hinder the legs from moving nimbly.

F) The Legs

In practising Chen Style Taijiquan, special care must be given to the position and motion of the legs which are of great importance to the stability and balance of the body, as well as the flexibility and deftness of the upper limbs. You should bend or extend the knee naturally and smoothly according to the special requirement of the action. The hips should be lowered and relaxed, and the crotch should be held open and rounded, therefore ensuring agile footwork, big strides, smooth shifting of the weight and high kicks of the feet. You might keep the hips at knee level as far as possible while forming a bow stance or a horse-riding stance. However, you can appropriately adjust the height of the stance in accordance with your age and physical conditions.

2) Body Technique

All the movements of taijiquan conform to the normal physiological states of muscles and joints. Therefore, you should try to obtain a sense of natural yielding, not that of awkwardness, throughout the whole process of practice. Regardless of the pace of a movement, the height of a stance and the direction in which the torso turns, the body should remain upright, natural, poised, relaxed and dexterous, but not stiff, full, feeble and buoyant. In detail, the body technique of Chen Style Taijiquan in common use includes the following.

A) Lifting of the Flank

This relates to the slight up-and-down relative motion of the flanks, and it actually refers to the shifting of the torso weight between the left and the right parts of the waist, which results in the transformation of emptiness and solidness of the flanks, hips and legs. When you place your torso weight on the left part of the lumbar section with the left flank set firm on the left hip, and thereby on the left leg, the right flank is slightly lifted, as if the right part of the waist were propped up by the left part. In this condition, the left part of the waist is solid, the left hip and the left leg are solid too; yet the right part of the waist , together with the right hip and leg, is empty and vice versa.

B) Turning of the Torso

Turn your torso to the left or to the right with the hips almost stationary. Keep the head erect and confirm its motion to the turn of the torso which is carried out with the lumbar and abdominal muscles as the active contractors. For instance, if you turn your torso to the left, you should face the left side; and if you turn your torso to the right, you should correspondingly face the right side.

C) Rolling of the Waist (circling of the torso)

Initiated by the lumbar and abdominal

muscles, the upper body rolls round the lumbar spine with the torso straight and the hips almost stationary, moving in a tiny horizontal clockwise or counterclockwise until it resumes the previous position. Although it is actually an action of the torso, it is called "rolling of the waist" because of the important role which the waist plays in the movement.

It is often difficult for beginners to distinguish between the application of lumbar and abdominal muscles and the motion of the hips while doing Chen Style Taijiquan, therefore beginners are subject to such a mistake as only turning hips with the waist still. In order to use the lumbar and abdominal muscles freely and independently to accomplish this action, you can first practise as follows: Stand upright; apply only the lumbar and abdominal muscles to move the upper body leftward then rightward, with the torso erect and the hips not turning. After you get the essentials, you can proceed with the complete "rolling of the waist".

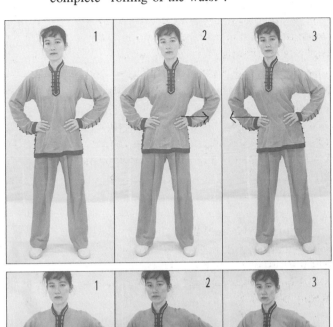

The rolling of waist

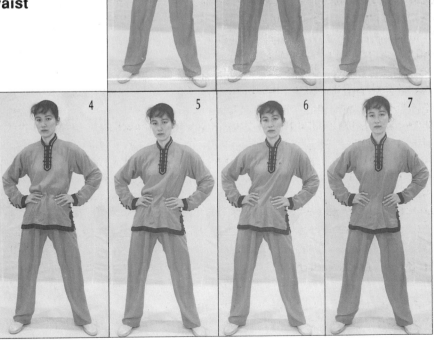

15

3) Eye Technique

Eyes are the windows of the soul, expressing the internal consciousness and incarnating the ingeniousness of the movements. Ancient martial arts regarded the expression in one's eyes as a means of first deterrent in actual combat. The importance of the eye technique is rightly delineated by a Wushu jargon, "Of a hundred boxing skills, the eye is the vanguard." If one is unable to apply eye technique correctly in practice, it is difficult for him to display his prowess and smartness, and he wants some exercise to improve his skill. You should open your eyes naturally to look horizontally at the attacking hand or in the main direction of attack, with side sight showing consideration for surroundings. The eyes should be well coordinated with the movements of the hands, legs and the torso. Keep your facial expression natural, earnest, calm and resourceful. Do not slant the head, nor cast a sidelong glance or stare angrily with the eyes wide-opened. The methods in detail are as follows.

During the transitional process between forms or in the phase the arms are in motion, eyes should follow the main attacking hand (usually the hand in front).

In a fixed posture with a hand in front of the face, you should look through the tip of the middle finger forward. If one hand goes to the left and the other to the right, or one up and the other down, you should look horizontally to the front.

4) Hand Patterns

A) The Fist: Close the four fingers and fold them into the hollow of the hand naturally. Bend the thumb and place its first phalange over the second phalanges of the forefinger and the middle finger.

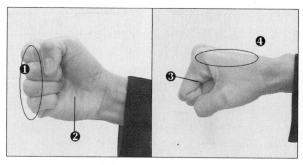

❶ The forefist   ❸ The eye of fist
❷ The centre of fist   ❹ The back of fist

B) The Palm (the corrugated palm): Stretch the fingers naturally. Cup the hand with the thumb and the little finger slightly curved up from both sides, and the other three expanded in sequence, thus shaping the hand into a concave palm like a tile.

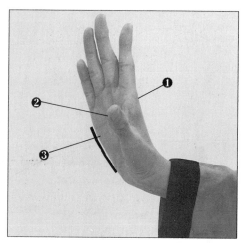

❶The back of palm
❷The hollow of palm
❸The edge of palm (the little finger side of the hand)
Standing Palm: Hold the palm with the

wrist dropped and the fingers pointing upward.

Upward Palm: Hold the palm with the hollow of the hand facing upward.

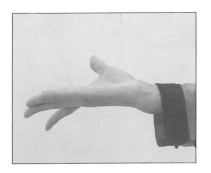

Downward palm: Hold the palm with the hollow of the hand facing downward.

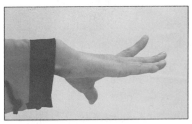

Thwartwise Palm: Hold the hand thwartwise with the wrist bent to the ulna, the hollow of the hand facing downward, and the force concentrated on the little finger side.

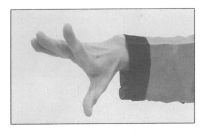

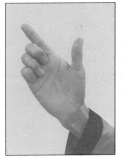

Finger Palm: Hold the hand with the thumb and the forefinger stretched out, and the other three naturally rolled up.

C) The Hook: Crook the wrist to form a hook with the tips of the thumb and the

forefinger brought together, and the other three naturally bunched up.

5) Hand Methods

Although Chen Style Taijiquan is imbued with manifold hand skills, the arms actions can be sorted out into four fundamental modes.

A) Inward Rotation: The arm (especially the forearm) rotates inward, making the thumb side of the palm turn in the direction of the hollow of the hand.

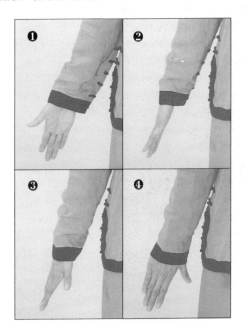

B) Outward Rotation: The arm (especially the forearm) rotates outward, making the thumb side of the palm turn in the direction of the back of the hand.

(See the photographs on next page)

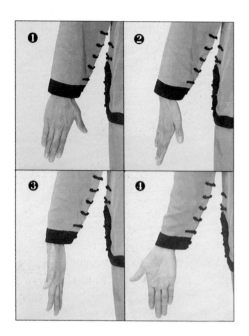

C) Folding: The "Boxing Manual" handed down by predecessors makes it a rule that "There must be a fold between travelling to and fro, and a transition between advance and retreat." Here, "folding" does not refer to a bend at some joint, but a turn in the path of a special part of the body. If a movement has a path first in one direction and then in the opposite direction, you should conduct a "folding" for the turn in the path so as to change the direction flowingly, as if inserting a curve to connect two line segments smoothly. So a Wushu jargon runs: "Intend to rise, descend first; Wish to move leftward, go rightward beforehand. " The way of "folding" is that : When the previous movement reaches its end and the next is in another direction, you should conduct a small circular turn, moving

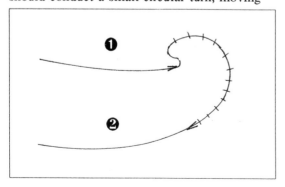

first in the previous direction and then transforming smoothly to the next. The "folding" actions of arms, especially the wrist, are quite clear. However, only with the aid of the twisting at waist, can "folding" be consummately manifested.

D) Twining: Spiral twining or reeling, in short, is a kind of unique motion with power passing through spirally from its root to the special part of the body in power order.

Spiral twining is the result of coordination of all parts of the body. It takes shape with the continuous rotations of the legs, torso and arms, and the twists at ankles, waist and wrists. Explained in detail, a spiral twining is such an action that the arm rotates round its own axis while it is travelling in an arc through space, just as the earth revolves both round the sun and on its own axis. The earth moves in a certain path and at a certain speed, yet the movements of the arms in doing Chen Style Taijiquan are changeable both in path and at speed. In other words, to fulfil the requirement of "Once any part in motion, nothing would remain still", the hand should cooperate harmoniously with the legs and the torso, should move and turn uninterruptedly, thereby displaying various twining throughout the whole process.

In many books of old days, the three-twining is explained as "smooth twining" and "reverse twining". Speaking scientifically, smooth twining is the one with the arm rotating outward; correspondingly, reverse twining is the one with the arm rotating inward. In order to make it simple and easy to learn, I will describe twining actions in terms of arm rotation in this book, not the smooth or reverse twining.

The drills in twining differ from each other. The following is one of the basic exercises handed down from ancient times:

Rotate the arm (especially the hand) inward or outward while the hand is moving along the path of a Taiji-diagram.

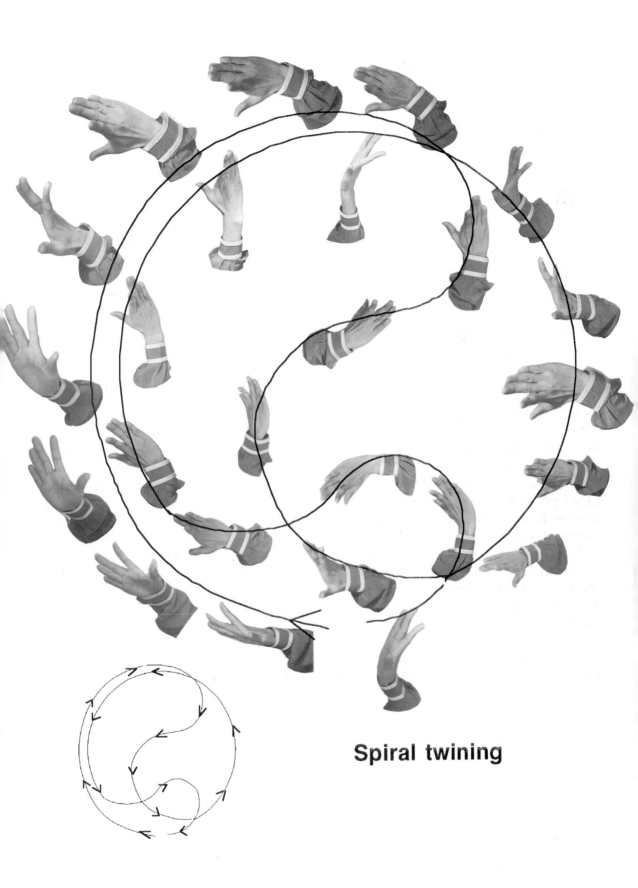

Spiral twining

6) Stances

A) Bow Stance: Stand upright with one foot in front and the other at the back about a big step apart. Bend the front leg at the knee and drop to a half squat, with the toes turned

slightly inward, the thigh almost level and thew knee in a straight line directly above the toes. Straighten the rear leg naturally with the toes obliquely pointing outward. Place both soles fully on the floor.

B) Horse-riding Stance: Stand upright with the feet to the sides about three foot length apart and the toes pointing forward.

Bend both legs at the knee and drop to a half squat with both thighs almost level.

C) Half Horse-riding Stance: Stand upright with one foot in front and the other at the back about three foot lengths apart. Bend the rear leg at the knee and drop to a high squat with the hips a bit higher than knee level

and the toes pointing outward. Bend the front leg slightly at the knee with the toes a little turned inward. Keep the weight mainly on the rear leg.

D) Dominated-horse-riding Stance: Stand upright with the feet to the sides about three and a half foot lengths apart. Bend both legs at

the knee and drop to a half squat but with the hips a bit higher than knee level. Keep the hips lowered and the buttocks slightly in. When you place the weight predominantly on the right leg, you form a "right-dominated horse-riding stance"; while you keep the weight predominantly on the left leg, you form a "left-

dominated horse-riding stance".

E) Empty Stance: a) Stand upright with one in front. Bend the rear leg at the knee and drop to a half squat with the thigh almost level, the sole fully on the floor and the toes obliquely pointing outward. Keep the weight on

the rear leg. Bend the front leg slightly at the knee with the ankle extended and the toes resting emptily on the floor.

b) Stand on one leg with the sole of the foot fully placed on the floor to support the body. Place the other foot about 5 cm back and beside the front one with the sole or the ball resting emptily on the floor. Keep both legs at the knee.

F) One-knee-raised Stance: Stand upright on one leg with the knee extended. Raise the other leg with the knee bent and the foot naturally suspended.

One-knee-raised Stance

G) Crouch Stance: Stand with the feet a big step apart. Bend one leg at the knee and drop to a full squat with the thigh close to the

calf and the toes turned slightly outward. Stretch the other leg sideways with the toes turned inward. Place both soles fully on the floor.

H) Feet-together Stance: Stand upright with the feet together and the soles fully placed on the floor.

I) Dropping Splits: Stretch the front leg forward with the toes tilted up, and bend the rear leg at the knee to drop, until the back of the front leg, the inner side of the rear leg and the buttocks are placed on the floor. Keep the

torso erect.

7) Footwork

A) Forward Step: The rear foot takes a step forward, or the front foot advances half a step.

B) Backward Step: The front foot takes a step backward.

C) Retreat Step: The front foot or the rear foot takes a step backward.

D) Serial Forward Steps: One foot takes a step forward, then the other foot advances.

E) Front Cross-step: One foot lands in front of and across the weight-bearing foot.

F) Back Cross-step: One foot lands behind and across the weight-bearing foot.

G) Jumping Step: As the front foot drives down on the floor to leap forward, the rear foot swings forward and then lands in front.

H) Toe-out Step: Turn toes outward while the foot lands in front.

I) Toe-in Step: Turn toes inward while the

foot lands in front.

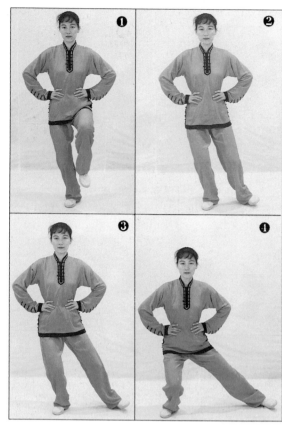

J) Foot-twisting: Turn toes inward or outward using the heel as an axis, or turn the heel using the ball of the foot. These actions are usually employed while shifting the weight in doing taiji exercises.

The above-mentioned steps are the commonly used fundamental footwork of taijiquan which have been introduced in Chinese Martial Arts Series 2 — T'ai-chi Swordplay. In addition, Chen Style Taijiquan is possessed of some distinct footwork as follows.

K) Dragging Step: Immediately after the front foot advances, the rear foot follows up with the knee bent, the toes turned out and the

whole sole scraping along the floor.

L) Lifting Step: With one leg supporting the body, the other foot rises swiftly with the knee bent and then lands on the floor again.

M) Shoveling Step: Squat down on one leg with the knee bent. The other foot shovels out with the knee gradually extended and the inner

side of the heel gently scraping along the floor.

N) Stamp: (See photos 17-18, 69-70 and 301-303 at Thirty-six, or see photos 25-26, 132-133, 517-519 at Fifty-six Movements Taijiquan)

O) Transition Step: During the process of shifting weight while moving forward or backward, the path of the foot is not a straight line, but a smooth arc. For instance, when you takes a step backward, the front foot should first move close to the inner side of the rear one, then step obliquely to the rear, with the ball of the foot gently scraping along the floor throughout the entire proceeding.

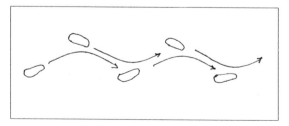

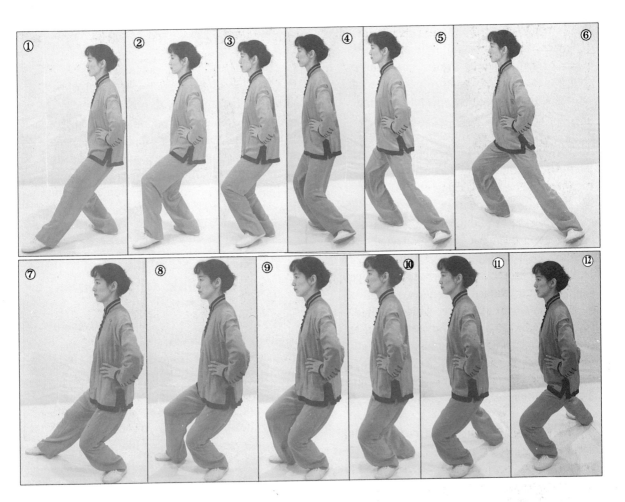

4. Main Points for Practice

1) Tranquil Mind, Relaxed Body and Erect Bearing

"Tranquil mind" means that while in practice, you should be calm, getting rid of any distracting thought and concentrating your attention on the details of the movements. With the mind directing all the actions you should strive to manifest the implications of attack and defence through the absorbed spirit, so that the so-called state of "body goes where spirit reaches" and "combining inside and outside into one" can be achieved.

"Relaxed body" indicates that the postures should be natural, with all muscles, joints and ligaments comfortably relaxed, so that every part of the limbs and trunk can move freely. With the consciousness guiding the breathing and the motion, all movements should be smooth and fluid. You must see that stiffness and awkwardness do not appear. On the other hand, you should keep your performance from being flaccid or lacking in strength.

"Erect bearing" refers to the position of the lumber spine. It requires the torso to be erect, not bending forward or backward, nor inclining to either side, no matter how the movements change.

2) Opening and Closing, Emptiness and Solidness

The coordination of internal and external in taijiquan is noticeable with the opening-closing change and the emptiness-solidness transformation. "Opening and Closing" are the external forms of actions directed by the internal spirit. Opening means expansion or enlargement, while closing refers to restraint or contraction. Generally speaking, all the movements in the direction away from the centre of the torso such as stretching, expanding and rising belong to opening; and those in the direction toward the centre of the torso such as bending, contracting and falling belong to closing. For instance, when the chest expands by the extending of the arms, it is opening; and when the chest contracts by the withdrawal of the arms, it is closing.

"Emptiness and solidness" are two opposite states which go through every movement of taijiquan. Viewed as whole, the completed posture is solid, while the process of motion is empty. When an action is analyzed partially, the leg which bears most of the weight is solid, while the leg which moves or assists to support the body is empty; the limbs which express the main substance of the motion are solid, while the limbs which play merely a subsidiary role are empty. From the angle of consciousness, if you focus your attention on the right hand, the right hand is solid, thereby the left hand is empty. Likewise, if you concentrate your awareness on the hollow of the hand, this side of the palm is solid, and the back of the palm is empty.

Opening and closing, emptiness and solidness are relative but ubiquitous. Of any two, if one is opening, the other is inevitably closing. Along with the progression of forms, it is always the same with emptiness and solidness, There is closing imbued in opening, and opening in closing; there is emptiness embodied in solidness, and solidness in emptiness. Generally speaking, they change constantly and gradually, from opening to closing, or from closing to opening; from emptiness to solidness, or from solidness to emptiness. However, in some movements of Chen Style Taijiquan, such as jump and strength discharge, the transformation of

emptiness-solidness should be accomplished with great speed.

The opening-closing change and the emptiness-solidness transformation should be naturally coordinated with breathing. In general, movements of opening, stretching, expanding and rising are usually accompanied by inspiration, while those of closing, bending, contracting and falling by expiration. You can readjust the cooperation of motion and respiration according to the requirement of a particular movement.

3) Be Nimble, Steady, Full of Vitality, and Sink Qi to Dantian

From beginning to end, all the movements, including those of expansion, contraction, advance and retreat, should be carried out nimbly and steadily, but not buoyantly or stagnantly. You should be full of vitality and able to apply your energy stream to promote actions. Be sure not to let your motion drift into looseness and slackness like a deflated rubber ball. The movements should look light and relaxed in appearance, but full of vigour in essence, as if the inner power may break forth at any moment.

To achieve this, you must abide by the principle of "Sinking Qi to Dantian". Here, the "Qi" means the vital energy stream and the "Dantian" refers to the acupuncture point just under the naval in the centre of the lower abdomen. That is to say, while in practice, with consciousness controlling all actions, you should direct your vital energy stream down to Dantian, so as to get a sense of substantiality in that part of the body. In Chen Style Taijiquan, much strength comes out from Dantian. So only in this way can you keep your stance firm and your movement steady, and avoid falling into such an awkward position as floating or losing roots.

4) Coordinate Upper and Lower

Halves, Combine Internal and External into One

Taijiquan is an overall physical training, requiring every part of the body to be in complete harmony. With the lumbar spine as the main axis of most actions, you should manage to coordinate the upper and the lower parts of the body, that is to say, the arms and the legs, and not to separate them into isolated ones. ir is often so described: "A single movement sets the whole body moving". When an action is finished, the legs, the torso, the arms and eyes must arrive at their right positions accurately at the same time.

In practising taijiquan, it is not enough to perform the movements correctly just by appearances. You must lay great emphasis on the internal elements, and use your consciousness to direct all bodily actions throughout the whole process so as to combine internal and external into one. But it is often difficult to reach such a state at the very beginning. Therefore, it is better to start with attention only paid to the correctness of your performance. After you acquire proficiency in performing the forms, you should manage to initiate the internal energy stream with the external actions. Then, you can go on to put special stress on the internal factors such as inner power, energy stream and internal motion, and gradually turn to conduct any movement from inside outward and direct the energy stream to promote actions. So the Wushu jargons run: "Internal motion guides external from, external form coincides with internal motion" and "without motion inside, no action outward". Therefore step by step, you can finally achieve a complete concordance of spirit and form, and manifest the integrative meaning of the movements.

5) Go Slow First, Quicken, Then Slow Down Again to Master Correct Variations in Speed

During the first phase of exercise, you should go as slow as possible rather than fast, because a slow pace can help you to lay a solid foundation, that is to say, to correct movements, to grasp forms accurately, to improve endurance gradually, and to develop firm and agile inner power. But you must remain vigorous, and concentrate your attention from beginning to end. Be sure not to be obtuse or rigid.

When you become rather skilled, you can gradually quicken the pace and shorten the time necessary for accomplishing a complete routine. But you should remain steady, not allowing your movements to become floating or fall into confusion.

Then, after you have a good command of the movements, you may slow down the pace again. But you must not be satisfied with an even pace, because it does not agree with the requirements of Chen Style Taijiquan. At this stage, you must strive to master the correct variations in speed, i.e. to alternate between high and low speeds. You should move slowly at any turn in the path of any part of the body. After you finish the turn, you should pick up speed gradually. At the moment the special part of the body comes to a final position, the pace of your movement reaches its peak. Go round and begin again just in this way.

6) Stress Martial Morality, Persevere in Practice

Although most movements of Chen Style Taijiquan have implications of attack and defence, its function to improve one's health both in body and mind is of greater value to us. The practitioner should cultivate himself to be a moral person, to respect the teacher and love his friends, and to study diligently and train hard on purpose to build up his health. As a proverb runs: "having practised ten thousand times, the wonder will come out itself." Three years' exercise reaps first fruits, and nine years' practice receives great successes. What is most important is perseverance. If one works by fits and starts, as he goes fishing for three days and dries the nets for two, he will be unable to master taijiquan. Only with persistent practice can one understand the profundity and subtlety of taijiquan, and obtain its health-building effects in time.

Part 1
Chen style
Thirty-six Movements
Taijiquan

1. The Names of the Thirty-six Movements

Stage One

1. Opening Form
2. Buddha's Warrior Attendant Pounds with a Pestle and Mortar — Right
3. Clasp and Tie the Coat
4. White Crane Spreads Wings
5. Walk Obliquely and Twist Step
6. Lift and Retract
7. Wade Forward
8. Cover Hand and Thrust Fist
9. Push with Both Hands
10. Fist under Elbow

Stage Two

11. Step Back and Roll Arms
12. Step Back and Press Elbow
13. Part the Wild Horse's Mane — Right and Left
14. Golden Cock Stands on Single Leg — Left and Right
15. Six Sealings and Four Closings — Right
16. Single Whip — Left

Stage Three

17. Wave Hands Like Clouds
18. High Pat on Horse
19. Rub Instep — Right and Left
20. Kick with Right Foot
21. Punch with Body Draped Over
22. Lean with Back Twisted
23. Blue Dragon Goes Out of Water
24. White Ape Presents Fruit
25. Six Sealings and Four Closings — Left
26. Single Whip — Right

Stage Four

27. Double Stamps with Feet
28. Jade Girl Works at Shuttles
29. Beast's Head pose
30. Dragon on the Ground
31. Step Forward with Seven Stars
32. Step Back and Mount the Tiger
33. Turn Round and Swing Lotus
34. The Head-on Cannon
35. Buddha's Warrior Attendant Pounds with a Pestle and Mortar — Left
36. Closing Form

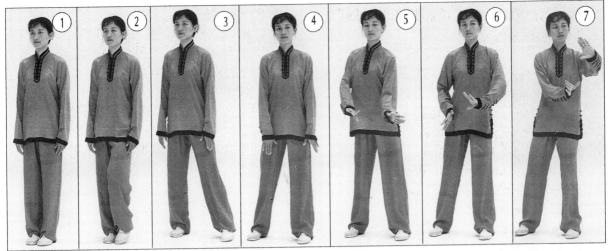

2. Performance of the Thirty-six Movements

Preparatory Form

(1)
Stand upright with your body naturally relaxed, feet together, arms hanging down. Keep calm and breathe naturally. Concentrate your attention and look horizontally forward.

(2 - 3)
Lift the left foot gently and move it to the left until your feet are about a shoulder-width apart and parallel to each other. Then, distribute your weight evenly on both legs.

Stage One
Form 1
Opening Form

(4)
Shift your weight slightly onto the ball of the left foot. Swing both arms in an arc to the front-left, with both wrists relaxed, the backs of the wrists protruding a little forward.

(5)
Shift your weight onto the heel of the right foot and turn your torso slightly to the right. Meanwhile, swing both arms rightward and slightly backward so that each hand draws a small circle respectively to the front-right of the abdomen, with the wrists extended, palms facing downward, fingers pointing to the front.

(6 - 7)
Shift your weight onto the ball of the left foot again and turn your torso slightly to the left. At the same time, swing both arms leftward, forward and upward to the chest level, with the elbows slightly bent. Look in the direction of the left hand.

(8 - 9)
Squat yourself down a little with both legs slightly bent, keeping your weight predominantly on the left leg. As your torso begins turning to the right, rotate the left arm outward and the right one inward so as to hold both hands crosswise, with the palms facing outward and the fingers pointing to the front-left. Then, with the toes of the right foot turned out using the heel as the pivot, the torso continues to turn to the right. Meanwhile, move your arms horizontally to the front-right, keeping the hands a shoulder-width apart.

Purpose: When the opponent thrusts his right fist into your chest, you can dodge the blow by

29

turning your torso swiftly to the right. Moreover, you can catch hold of his right wrist with your right hand and clasp his right upper arm with your left hand, pulling him to the rear-right. Therefore, the opponent is bound to lose his balance.

Form 2
Buddha's Warrior Attendant
Pounds with a Pestle and Mortar
— Right

(10 - 11)
Shift your weight completely onto the right leg with the knee further bent. Lift the left foot

slightly and then move it to the front-left with the inner side of the heel scraping along the floor. At the same time, push both your hands to the front-right.

(12)
Along with a twist of the torso, each hand revolves on its own wrist leftward, upward and rightward, drawing a small circle.

(13 - 16)
With the toes of the left foot slightly turned out, shift your weight gradually onto the left leg and turn your torso to the left. At the same time, both arms drop respectively. As the right foot moves a step forward with the ball first scraping along the floor and then resting gently on the floor to form a right empty stance, the right hand swings to the front of the right hip with the palm facing

the upper-front; while the left forearm revolves forward, upward and then backward, drawing a vertical circle before placing the hand crosswise upon the right forearm, the elbow bent and the palm facing obliquely backward.

(17 - 18)

Raise yourself slightly by straightening the left leg, and lift the right leg with the knee bent and the foot naturally suspended. At the same time, the left hand drops to the front of the abdomen with the palm facing upward and the fingers pointing to the right; while the right hand changes into a fist and comes up to the chest level with the centre of the fist facing upward. Without any pause, as you bent the left leg slightly to squat down, the right foot stamps on the floor forcibly. Meanwhile, the right fist smashes down into the left palm with the centre of the fist remaining upward.

Purpose: When the opponent thrusts his right fist into your left ribs, you can ward off the attack with your left arm, and strike him on the crotch with your right palm. You can then continue to wield your right fist upward, punching him on the chin.

Form 3
Clasp and Tie the Coat

(19 - 21)

Shift your weight slightly onto the right leg and turn your torso slightly to the left. Simultaneously, the left hand, holding the right fist in the palm, moves to the front of the left side of the waist. Then, with the right fist opened and both the arms rotating inward, raise your hands until they cross in front of the chest. Without any pause, the right hand moves upward, outward, downward and then inward, drawing a large circle until it gets to the front of the abdomen, the palm facing leftward; while the left hand drops and then continues to go outward, upward and inward to the front of the chest, the palm facing rightward. As both arms press inward from both sides with the elbows bent, shift your weight onto the left leg and lift the right foot.

(22)

The right foot lands and moves to the front-right with the inner side of the heel scraping along the floor, until it is three and a half foot lengths apart from the left one. In the meantime, turn your torso slightly to the left, with both arms continuing the inward motion.

(23)

Rotate the right forearm inward so as to hold a horizontal palm with the palm facing down and the elbow bent. Simultaneously, rotate the left arm outward until the palm is up and the back of the hand rests upon the right upper arm.

(24 - 26)

Turn your torso to the right and shift your weight rightward to form a right-dominated horse-riding stance (with the right leg slightly bent at the knee and the left leg naturally extended, keeping the weight predominantly on the right leg). At the same time, the right hand rises and then moves in a horizontal arc to the right with the wrist lowered to form a standing palm which faces the front-right with the fingertips at shoulder level; while the left hand drops to the front of the abdomen with the palm remaining upward.

Purpose: If the opponent thrusts his left fist into your chest, you can deflect the blow with your right arm. Then, with your left hand clasping his left wrist, you can step up, bumping him with your right shoulder or elbow, or swatting

him on the face with your right hand.

Form 4
White Crane Spreads Wings

(27 - 28)

Turn your torso to the left and shift your weight leftward. Meanwhile, with the left palm turned down, lower both hands and move them in an arc to the left.

(29)

Shift your weight onto the right leg again. Raise both arms and begin to swing them to the right with the palms facing outward and the fingers pointing to the left.

(30)

Following the turn of the torso, both hands move in a horizontal arc to the right. Then, with the toes of the left foot turned out, squat yourself down a little more. The left hand drops in the meantime.

(31 - 34)

Turn your torso to the left and shift your weight gradually onto the left leg. Bring the right foot forward with the ball scraping along the floor, and then place the toes gently on the floor next to the left heel. At the same time, the left hand goes to the left, then rises to the front of the chest, the arm bent, the palm facing rightward. Simultaneously, the right hand follows in a semicircle to the front of the abdomen, the arm slightly bent, the palm facing to the left. Both arms press

inward sharply and explosively from both sides.

(35 - 38)

As you bend the left leg a little more and turn your torso slightly to the left, the right foot takes a step to the front-right. Then, shift your weight forward onto the right leg and turn your torso slightly to the right again. The left foot follows up with the ball scraping along the floor until it rests gently on the floor next to the right foot, forming a left empty stance. At the same time, the right hand circles leftward, upward and rightward, from outside the left arm, to the front-right at head level, the arm rounded, the palm facing obliquely outward, the fingers pointing upward; while the left hand moves rightward, downward, and then leftward to the side of the left hip with the palm facing downward and the fingers point-

ing to the front.

Purpose: If the opponent thrusts his right fist into your belly, you can catch hold of his arm by seizing his wrist with your right hand and clasping his elbow with your left hand, and then pull him down. The moment he is attempting to withdraw, you can step up and swing your right arm upward and outward, causing him to fall.

Form 5
Walk Obliquely and Twist Step

(39 - 40)
Turn your torso slightly to the left before turning it back to the right. Following the turns of the torso, the right hand circles leftward, and downward, passing before the abdomen, then upward

to the right side at shoulder level, the palm facing the lower-rear; while the left hand swings backward, upward and round to the right with the arm bent. As your weight is shifted completely onto the right leg, lift the left foot.

(41)
Without any pause, the left foot takes a step to the front-left with the inner side of the heel scraping

along the floor. As the foot is set firm, turn your torso slightly to the right. At the same time, the right hand pushes a bit further out with the fingers pointing to the front-left; while the left hand continues to move to the front of the right shoulder.

(42 - 45)
Turn your torso to the left and shift your weight

34

onto the left leg with the toes of the left foot turned out. Simultaneously, the left hand moves downward and leftward then rises to the front-left with the arm slightly bent, the fingertips brought together and the hand crooked at the wrist, thus forming a hook. In the meantime, the right hand goes upward with the arm bent, and then moves forward until it gets close to the left wrist.

(46 - 48)

Rotate the right forearm inward so as to turn the palm down. Along with the rightward turn of the torso, the right hand then moves horizontally to the front-right at shoulder level, with the shoulder lowered, the elbow dropped, the palm facing forward.

Purpose: If the opponent launches an attack on your chest with his right hand, you can grip his arm with your right hand and pull it down to the right. Then, you can step toward his rear with your left foot, bumping him with your left shoulder or elbow and strike him on the face with your right palm.

35

Form 6
Lift and Retract

(49 - 50)

As you turn your torso to the left, the left hand, changed back from a hook to a palm, revolves counterclockwise on the wrist so as to turn the palm out, and then moves to the front of the left part of the chest with the palm facing rightward; while the right hand circles downward and leftward until it comes beneath the left forearm at abdomen level with the palm facing the left.

(51 - 53)

Shift your weight backward onto the right leg and draw the left foot back to a position 30 cm in front of the right one with the ball scraping along the floor, thus forming a left empty stance with the left leg slightly bent at the knee. At the same time, rotate both arms outward to turn the palms up, and withdraw both hands to the front of the abdomen with the left hand a little ahead and rightward one about 10 cm apart from the stomach and beside the left forearm. Set your eyes on the left palm.

(54 - 56)

Shift your weight completely onto the right leg. As you straighten the right leg to stand up, raise the left leg with the knee bent. Meanwhile, with the arms rotating inward respectively so as to

36

turn the palms down, both hands push forward and downward, the fingers pointing to the front.

Purpose: If the opponent launches an attack on your chest with his right hand, you can bend his arm backward by seizing his wrist with your right hand and clasping his elbow with your left hand and pressing inward from both sides. When the opponent is attempting to withdraw, you can raise your left knee to bump against his crotch and shove him to the ground with both your hands.

Form 7
Wade Forward

(57 - 58)
Bend the right leg to squat down and turn your torso to the right. Simultaneously, the left foot takes a step to the front-left with the inner side of the heel scraping along the floor. Both hands circle downward and rightward, passing before the abdomen to the right side.

(59 - 60)
Without any pause, turn your torso to the left and shift your weight onto the left leg. At the same time, both hands continue to rise sideways up with the arms bent, and then push forward, the left palm facing backward, the right hand clinging to the left wrist with the little finger side ahead and the palm facing the left.

(61 - 62)
As you turn your torso slightly to the left and bring the right foot forward next to the left one, rotate both arms inward to turn the palms down.

(63 - 65)
As the right foot takes a step to the front-right, shift your weight onto the right leg to form a right-dominated horse-riding stance. At the same time, raise both hands slightly upward, and then separate them until each hand forms a standing palm diagonally to the side with the fingertips at nose level. Set your eyes on the right palm.

Purpose: If the opponent thrusts his right fist into your chest, you can deflect the blow by dragging his arm to the right side with your right hand. When he withdraws his arm, you can strike

him on the chest with both your hands. The moment he is attempting to retreat, you can step up, bumping him with your right elbow and swatting him on the face with your right hand.

Form 8
Cover Hand and Thrust Fist

(66 - 67)
As your torso turns slightly to the left, the right hand revolves on the wrist leftward, backward and rightward, drawing a small horizontal circle, to turn the palm up.

(68)
Shift your weight onto the left leg and roll up the fingers of the right hand from little finger to

thumb successively to make a fist.

(69)

As you raise the right leg with the knee bent, rotate the right arm inward and bend the elbow so as to wield the right fist down. The left hand moves upward, inward and downward in the meantime, until it rests upon the right forearm with the fingers pointing to the upper-right.

(70)

As your torso slightly turns to the right, the right foot stamps on the floor forcibly. Meanwhile, the right fist, accompanied by the left hand, continues to strike down, passing before the chest to the front of the abdomen, the forefist down and the eye of the fist facing backward.

(71)

The left foot takes a step to the front-left with the

inner side of the heel scraping along the floor.

(72 - 74)

Shift your weight onto the left leg and turn your torso to the left. Meanwhile, lower both hands and separate them with the right fist opened. Each hand then circles outward, upward and inward to the front of the chest.

(75 - 76)

As your torso twists slightly to the right, the right hand clenches into a fist and withdraws to the front of the left part of the chest with the arm bent and the centre of the fist facing upward. Meanwhile, with the thumb and the forefinger extended, and the other three together rolled up in the hollow of the hand, the left hand moves to the front of the left shoulder, the arm slightly bent

39

and the palm facing upward.

(77 - 78)

Turn your torso swiftly to the left with the right leg straightened so as to form a left bow stance. In the meantime, with the arm rotating inward, the right fist thrusts straight ahead at chest level, the centre of the fist turned down; while the left hand withdraws to the left side with the hand

pattern unchanged and the palm gently touching the abdomen. Set your eyes on the right fist.

Purpose: If the opponent thrusts his right fist into your chest, you can press his right arm with your left arm to deflect the blow, and then thrust your right fist into his chest.

Form 9
Push with Both Hands

(79 - 80)

As your torso turns slightly to the left, open the right fist and lower the hand to the front of the abdomen with the palm facing downward. Without any pause, turn your torso slightly to the right. Meanwhile, rotate the right arm outward

and raise the left hand so that both hands overlap with the back of the left hand against the inner side of the right wrist, both palms facing backward. Then, both hands together push to the upper-front-right at chest level.

(81 - 84)

Turn your torso to the left with the toes of the left foot turned out, and shift your weight onto the

left leg. The right foot then takes a step forward, passing beside the inner side of the left one with the ball scraping along the floor, until the sole gently touches the floor in front. Along with the turn of the torso, rotate the right forearm inward. Both hands then circle downward, and then forward and upward to the front-right at shoulder level with the arms rotating outward and the palms facing upward.

(85 - 86)

As the right foot goes half a step forward, rotate both arms inward and bend the elbows, withdrawing both hands to the front of the chest with the palms facing obliquely each other.

(87 - 89)

Shift your weight forward onto the right leg. The left foot follows up with the ball scraping along

the floor, until the sole gently rests on the floor behind the right heel. Meanwhile, both hands push forward at chest level, with the fingers pointing upward and the palms still facing each other obliquely. Look straight ahead.

Purpose: If the opponent launches an attack on your chest with his left hand, you can bend his elbow backward by gripping his wrist and pull-

ing it to the lower-right with your left hand, and pressing his elbow to the upper-left with your right hand. The moment he is attempting to retract, you can step up to punch him on the chest with both your hands.

(94) (95) (96) (97) (98)

Form 10
Fist under Elbow

(90 - 91)

As your torso slightly turns to the right, rotate the right forearm outward and withdraw the right hand to the front of the waist with the palm facing upward. Meanwhile, the left hand pushes forward from above the right hand, the palm facing downward and the fingers pointing to the front-right. Look in the direction of the left hand.

(92 - 93)

As your torso slightly turns to the left, the left hand circles rightward, backward and leftward until it goes to the front of the abdomen with the arm rotating outward to turn the palm up. Meanwhile, the right hand pushes leftward and forward from above the left arm, with the arm rotating inward to turn the palm down. Set your eyes on the right hand.

(94 - 95)

As your torso turns slightly to the right, the left hand continues to circle leftward, upward and rightward until it gets to the front of the torso; while the right hand moves in a vertical arc upward, rightward and downward.

(96)

Turn your torso slightly to the left. Hold the left hand in front with the wrist sunk to form a

standing palm, the fingertips slightly higher than the eyebrow level, the palm facing the front-right. Simultaneously, the right hand continues to move leftward until it pauses just under the left elbow at abdomen level, with the palm clenched into a fist, the eye of the fist on top. Set your eyes on the left hand.

Purpose: Wave your left arm to the right to fend off a blow, and thrust your right fist from under the left elbow to punch the opponent in the abdomen or on the ribs.

Stage Two
Form 11
Step Back and Roll Arms

(97 - 99)

Shift your weight onto the right leg and bend the leg a little more to squat down. The left foot rises and takes a step to the rear-left. As the torso slightly turns to the left, the right fist returns to a palm and stretches forward and upward from above the left arm, the palm facing upward. Both arms then rotate inward. As you form a right-dominated horse-riding stance, the right hand continues to circle to the right at shoulder level with the palm facing the lower-front and the finger pointing to the front-left; while the left hand drops to the front of the abdomen with the palm facing downward and the fingers pointing

to the front-right. Look in the direction of the right hand.

(100 - 101)
As you shift your weight onto the left leg and turn your torso to the right, the left hand continues to circle leftward and upward. Both arms then extend and rotate outward swiftly and explosively at shoulder level to turn the palms up.

(102 - 105)
With the rebounding force, shift your weight completely onto the left leg and turn your torso further to the right. At the same time, the right foot takes a step to the rear-right, passing beside the inner side of the left one and scraping along the floor, to form a left-dominated horse-riding stance. As the right hand withdraws to the front of the abdomen with the arm bent and the palm facing the lower-front, the left arm rolls up. The left hand then pushes forward passing beside the left cheek and from above the right arm, the palm facing the front-right.

43

(106)   (107)   (108)

(106 - 108)

As you shift your weight onto the right leg and continue to turn the torso to the right, the right hand circles rightward and upward. Both arms then extend and rotate outward swiftly and explosively to turn the palms up.

(109 - 112)

With the rebounding force, shift your weight completely onto the right leg and turn your torso swiftly to the left. At the same time, the left foot takes a step to the rear-left, passing beside the inner side of the right one and scraping along the floor, to form a right-dominated horse-riding stance. As the left hand withdraws to the front of the abdomen with the arm bent and the palm

(109)   (110)   (111)   (112)

facing the lower-front, the right arm rolls up. The right hand then pushes forward passing beside the right cheek and from above the left arm until it gets to the front-right with the palm facing outward.

Purpose: Pull the opponent's attacking arm backward with your withdrawing hand, forcing him to lose his balance, and strike the opponent

on the throat or on the chest with your forward-pushing hand while you step back, thus using defense as a means of attack.

44

Form 12
Step Back and Press Elbow

(113 - 114)

As your torso turns to the right, press the left knee inward and close the hips, keeping the weight predominantly on the right leg. In the meantime, the left hand moves in a vertical arc leftward, upward, forward and rightward, until it gets to the front of the left part of the chest at nose level, with the palm facing the front-right and the fingers pointing to the front-left; while the right hand circles rightward, downward and leftward, until it goes underneath the inner side of the left elbow at abdomen level, with the palm facing the left.

(115)

Bend the left arm and rotate the forearm inward so that the left hand presses down to the front of the abdomen. The left palm then turns up again. Meanwhile, the right hand goes up from inside the left arm to the chest level, with the arm bent and the forearm rotating inward so as to turn the palm down.

(116 - 117)

Shift your weight onto the left leg and draw the right foot back with the ball scraping along the floor. Simultaneously, both arms twine round. The right hand moves forward, downward and backward until it gets to the front of the abdomen with the palm turned up; while the left hand rises from inside the right arm to the chest level with the arm bent and the palm facing downward.

45

(118)

The right foot takes a step backward with a thump on setting the sole on the floor. Shift your weight backward onto the right leg quickly to form a semi-horse-riding stance. At the same time, the left hand cuts to the front-left at chest level with the palm crosswise and facing downward, the force concentrated on the little finger side of the hand; while the right hand withdraws to the front of the waist with the palm still facing upward. Set your eyes on the left hand.

Purpose: If the opponent launches an attack with his right hand, you can catch hold of his wrist and twist his arm outward with your right hand, and then press his elbow down with your left forearm or palm while you step back and withdraw your right hand.

Form 13
Part the Wild Horse's Mane — Right and Left

(119 - 120)

While you continue to shift your weight onto the right leg and turn your torso to the right with the toes of the left foot turned inward, the left hand drops, and the right hand moves rightward and upward.

(121 - 123)

As your torso continues to turn round to the right, shift your weight back onto the left leg. Then, raise the right leg with the knee bent. At the same time, the right hand circles rightward, backward, downward, and then rises passing beside the

46

outer side of the right thigh to the front at shoulder level; while the left hand goes rightward, forward and then, with the forearm rotating inward, moves upward and leftward until it gets to the left side at a level slightly higher than the shoulder, the palm facing outward. Look in the direction of the right hand.

(124 - 126)
Bend the left leg to squat yourself down. Lower the right foot and move it further to the front-right with the heel scraping along the floor before the sole is set firm. Then, shift your weight forward onto the right leg to form a right-dominated horse-riding stance. Meanwhile, with a twist of the torso, the right hand stretches explosively to the front-right. The left hand drops

a little. Set your eyes on the right hand.

(127-129)
Shift your weight onto the right leg with the toes of the right foot turned out, and raise the left leg with the knee bent. As your torso turns slightly to the left and then back to the right, the right hand revolves counterclockwise on the wrist. The right arm then moves to the right side at shoulder level with the palm facing outward and the fin-

gers pointing to the front-left. At the same time, the left hand drops and then rises passing beside the outer side of the thigh to the front at shoulder level, the palm facing the upper-left and the fingers pointing to the front-left.

(130 - 132)
Bend the right leg to squat down. Lower the left foot and move it further to the front-left with the

47

heel scraping along the floor before the sole is set firm. Then, shift your weight forward onto the left leg to form a left-dominated horse-riding stance. Meanwhile, with a twist of the torso, the left hand stretches explosively to the front-left. The right hand drops a little. Set your eyes on the left hand.

Purpose (take the right form as an example): When the opponent launches an attack with his left fist, you can invalidate the blow by deflecting his arm upward and to the rear-left. Then, you can place your right foot behind the opponent's leg to control him. The moment he is attempting to retreat, you can stretch your right arm under his armpit to tumble him down with your arm and shoulder.

Form 14
Golden Cock Stand on Single Leg — Left and Right

(133 - 135)
As you shift your weight slightly to the left and then back to the right, the torso twists slightly to the left and then back to the right correspondingly. Meanwhile, with the arm bent and the palm turned up, each hand revolves on its own wrist leftward, backward and rightward, then moves to the front-right with the palm facing obliquely downward. After that, turn your torso

to the left swiftly and shift your weight onto the left leg, with the right leg straightened, the knee pressing inward, the hips closed, thus forming a left bow stance. At the same time, both hands press downward and leftward until the left hand gets to the front of the abdomen, and the right hand to the front of the right hip, with the wrist sunk, palms facing the lower-front, and fingers pointing to the front-right.

(136 - 137)
As your torso slightly twists to the left, both hands circle leftward, forward and upward. Without any pause, turn your torso to the right again and shift your weight slightly to the right. Both hands continue to move to the right.

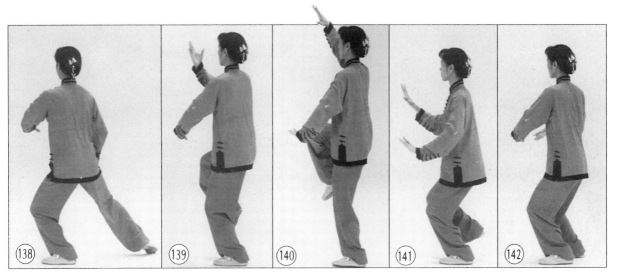

(138)

As you shift your weight to the left, both hands continue to circle downward and eftward.

(139 - 140)

Turn your torso to the left and shift your weight completely onto the left leg. Bring the right foot next to the left one with the ball scraping along the floor. Then, as you straighten the left leg to stand up, raise the right leg with the knee bent. At the same time, the left hand presses down to the side of the left hip with the palm facing downward; while the right hand penetrates upward from inside the left arm with the palm facing the torso. On passing before the face, the right forearm rotates inward to turn the palm out. The right hand continues to stretch to the upper-right with the fingers pointing upward.

(141 - 142)

Bend the left leg to squat yourself down. The right foot drops and stamps on the floor about 10 cm apart from the left one. Meanwhile, with the right hand slightly lowered and the left one slightly raised, both hands together press downward and forward, the palms facing downward and the fingers pointing to the front.

(143)
Turn your torso slightly to the left and shift your weight onto the left leg. Bend the left leg to squat down a little more while the right foot takes a step sideways. Meanwhile, both hands circle rightward, upward and leftward, until the left hand gets to the front-left at shoulder level, and the right hand to the front of the chest, with both palms facing the front-left and the fingers point-

ing to the front-right.

(144 - 146)
Shift your weight completely onto the right leg and bring the left foot next to the right one with the ball scraping along the floor. In the meantime, the right hand presses down with the forearm rotating inward to turn the hand to a crosscut palm; while the left hand circles leftward and

downward, passing beside the left hip, and then penetrates upward from inside the right arm, with the forearm rotating outward so as to turn the palm backward.

(147 - 148)
Without any pause, as you straighten the right leg to stand up, raise the left leg with the knee bent. At the same time, the right hand continues to

press to the side of the right hip with the palm facing downward; while the left hand continues to stretch to the upper-left with the fingers pointing upward and the forearm rotating inward to turn the palm out.

Purpose (take the left form as an example):
When the opponent thrusts his right fist into your ribs, you can deflect the blow by pressing his arm

50

down with your left hand. Then, you can raise your right knee to strike his crotch and thrusts your right hand into his throat or face.

Form 15
Six Sealings and Four Closings — Right

(149 - 150)
Bend the right leg to squat down. Lower the left foot and place it to the rear on the floor to form a right bow stance. At the same time, the left hand drops to the front at chin level with the forearm rotating outward so that the palm faces the upper-rear and the fingers point to the upper-front. Simultaneously, the right hand stretches from above the left palm to the upper-front at head level, the palm facing obliquely downward and the fingers pointing to the upper-front. Set your eyes on the right hand.

(151 - 153)
Shift your weight to the left leg while turning your torso to the left. Meanwhile, both hands move downward and slightly leftward, then rise with the arm rotating outward and pause promptly at chest level, the right palm facing upward and the left one facing obliquely backward.

(154 - 156)
The right foot advances half a step. As the torso turns to the right, bend both arms. Each hand revolves outward on its own wrist so as to move the hand above the shoulder with the palm facing the upper-front and the fingers pointing to the upper-rear. Look to the lower-front-right.

(157 - 159)

Shift your weight onto the right leg. Bring the left foot forward with the ball scraping along the floor and then rest it emptily on the floor next to the right one. Meanwhile, with both arms rotating inward, both hands press out, passing beside the cheeks, to the lower-front-right at abdomen level, the palms facing obliquely each other. Set your eyes on the hands.

Purpose: if the opponent launches an attack on your chest with both his hands, you can part his arms in the middle with both your hands to deflect the blow. Then, you can step up with your right foot and strike him on the chest or in the abdomen with your palms.

Form 16
Single Whip — Left

(160 - 161)

As you turn your torso slightly to the right and shift your weight slightly onto the left leg, the right hand withdraws to the right side of the waist with the palm turned up and the fingers pointing

to the front; while the left hand pushes forward from above the right one with the palm facing the lower-front.

(162 - 164)

Turn your torso slightly to the left and shift your weight onto the right leg. Simultaneously, the left hand withdraws to the front of the abdomen with the palm turned up and the fingers pointing

to the right; while the right hand changes into a hook and stretches from above the left palm to the upper-right at shoulder level, the tip of the hook pointing to the left. Look in the direction of the right hook.

(165)
Squat down a little more on the right leg. Lift the left foot and move it to the left side with the heel scraping along the floor until it is three and a half foot lengths apart from the right one.

(166 - 167)
Set the left foot firm on the floor. While shifting your weight to the left leg, turn your torso slightly to the left with the toes of the right foot slightly turned inward.

(168)
Without any pause, turn your torso to the right and shift your weight onto the right leg again. Simultaneously, the left hand stretches toward the right elbow with the palm facing upward and the fingers pointing to the front-right.

(169)
When the left hand gets close to the right elbow, rotate the forearm inward to turn the palm out.

(170 - 172)
Turn your torso to the left and shift your weight onto the left leg to form a left-dominated horse-riding stance. Meanwhile, the left hand moves in a horizontal arc to the front-left, keeping the waist relaxed, the shoulder lowered, the elbow dropped and the wrist sunk, thus forming a

53

standing palm at shoulder level. Eyes follow the left hand.

Purpose: If the opponent seizes you by your right wrist, you can press his wrist with your left hand and twist your right hand up, using the joined twisting force to break his wrist. The moment he is attempting to extricate himself, you can punch him on the chin or on the bridge of the nose with the top of your right hooked hand, and then slap him in the face backhanded with your left hand.

Stage Three
Form 17
Wave Hands like Clouds

(173)
Shift your weight further to the left with both arms relaxed. With the hook returned to a palm, the right hand revolves counterclockwise on its wrist with the forearm rotating outward so that the palm turns outward and the fingers point to the rear-right. In the meantime, the left hand also revolves counterclockwise on the wrist at shoulder level with the forearm rotating inward so that the palm turns outward and the fingers point to the front-right.

54

(174 - 176)

Turn your torso slightly to the right and shift your weight onto the right leg. Bring the left foot next to the right one quickly and rest the ball lightly on the floor. At the same time, the right hand moves in a circle upward, leftward, downward and rightward in succession, until it gets to the front-right again at a level slightly higher than the shoulder, the palm facing outward and the fin-

gers pointing to the front-left. Simultaneously, the left hand circles upward, leftward, downward and rightward, until it gets to the front of the abdomen with the palm facing outward and the fingers pointing to the front-left.

(177)

As you squat down a little more on the right leg, the left foot takes a step sideways. Simulta-

neously, both hands push slightly to the front-right.

(178 - 181)

Turn your torso slightly to the left and shift your weight onto the left leg. The right foot takes a back cross-step to the rear-left. Simultaneously, with the arm rotating inward, the left hand circles upward and leftward, the palm turned out and the

fingers pointing to the upper-right; while the right hand circles downward and leftward past the abdomen, the palm turned out and the fingers pointing to the front. Eyes follow the left hand.

(182 - 183)

Turn your torso slightly to the right. Set the right foot firm on the floor and shift your weight onto the right leg. The left foot then takes a step

sideways. Simultaneously, the right hand continues to rise and then moves in a horizontal arc passing before the chest to the right side at a level slightly higher than the shoulder, the palm turned out and the fingers pointing to the front-left. Meanwhile, the left hand circles downward and rightward, passing before the abdomen to the right side, the palm turned out and the fingers pointing to the front-left. Eyes follow the right hand.

hand circles upward, leftward, then rightward again with the forearm rotating outward, thus forming a standing palm in front of the chest with the palm facing the front-right. Simultaneously, the right hand moves downward and leftward to the front of the waist underneath the left elbow with the palm facing the left and the fingers pointing to the front. Eyes follow the left hand.

(184 - 188)
The same as those in Figures 178-183.

Purpose: If the opponent thrusts his hand into your chest or face, you can wave your left hand counterclockwise to seize him by the forearm or wrist. On pulling his arm leftward and downward, you can wield your right hand to strike him on the elbow or on the shoulder and back. You can also catch hold of the opponent's kicking leg and push it to the left so as to throw him down.

Form 18
High Pat on Horse

(189 - 191)
Turn your torso to the left and shift your weight onto the left leg with the toes turned out. Bring the right foot next to the left one with the toes resting on the floor. At the same time, the left

(192)
Cross your arms in front of the chest with the left one on top.

(193 - 195)
The right foot takes a step sideways. As you shift your weight onto the right leg to form a right-dominated horse-riding stance, rotate both arms inward and separate them from top to the sides.

Each hand then forms a standing palm diagonally to the side with the fingers slightly higher than shoulder level. Set your eyes on the right hand.

(196 - 200)
Twist your torso slightly to the right with the toes of the right foot turned inward. Extend both arms with the left arm slightly rotating inward to turn

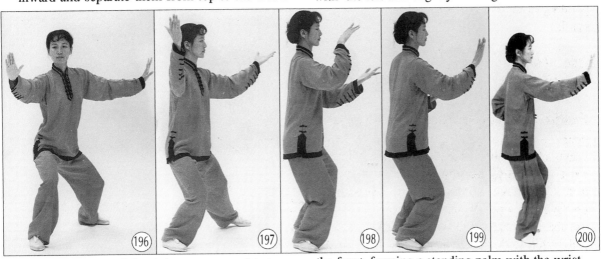

the palm down and the right arm outward to turn the palm up. Then, as you turn your torso to the left and shift your weight onto the right leg, the left foot moves backward, the ball scraping along the floor and then resting on the floor next to the right one. Simultaneously, the left hand withdraws to the left side of the waist with the palm turned up; while the right hand, with the arm rolling up pushes, passing beside the right ear to

the front, forming a standing palm with the wrist sunk and the fingers at nose level. Look in the direction of the right hand.

Purpose: If the opponent seizes you by your left wrist, you can coil your hand round his arm and withdraw the hand to drag him, and strike him on the face or on the chest with your right hand.

57

Form 19
Rub Instep — Right and Left

(201 - 204)

As your torso turns slightly to the left, the right hand drops to the front of the abdomen with the palm facing downward; while the left forearm rotates inward so that the palm nestles gently to the side of the abdomen.

(205 - 207)

Turn your torso slightly to the right. The right hand continues to move slightly to the left and then upward, the palm facing backward and the fingers pointing to the left; while the left hand rises. Both hands overlap in front of the chest with the back of the left hand against the inner

side of the right wrist. Both forearms then together push forward. Look straight ahead.

(208 - 211)

The left foot takes a step forward. Shift your weight onto the left leg to form a left bow stance. Simultaneously, the left hand circles downward, outward, upward and inward until it gets to the front of the chest, the arm slightly bent, the palm facing the right and the fingers pointing to the upper-front. Correspondingly, the right hand moves slightly upward with the forearm rotating inward, then goes outward, downward and inward until it gets to the front of the abdomen, the palm facing the left and the fingers pointing to the front.

58

(212 - 214)

Turn your torso slightly to the left and shift your weight completely onto the left leg. Raise the right leg and straighten the knee to kick forcibly to the upper-front with the toes pointed. Meanwhile, the right hand rises from inside the left arm, with the elbow bent and the forearm rotating inward, and then stretches forward and upward, slapping the instep of the right foot at shoulder level. The left hand circles rightward, downward and then sideways up to the left at head level in the meantime. Set your eyes on the right hand.

(215 - 216)

Lower the right foot onto the floor in front. Turn your torso slightly to the right and shift your weight onto the right leg to form a right bow

stance. Meanwhile, the right hand moves slightly outward, then presses inward again to the front of the chest with the palm facing the left and the fingers pointing to the upper-front. Simultaneously, the left hand circles downward, forward and inward to the front of the abdomen with the palm facing the right and the fingers pointing to the front.

(217 - 218)

The same as those in Figures 212-214, only reversing "right" and "left".

Purpose: (take the right form as an example): If the opponent launches an attack with his right hand, you can deflect the blow by pressing his arm downward and outward with your left hand.

Then, you can kick to the crotch with your right leg and strike him on the face with your right hand.

Form 20
Kick with Right Foot

(219 - 221)

Bend the right leg and lower the left foot onto the floor in front with the toes of the left foot turned inward. As you turn your torso to the right and shift your weight completely onto the left leg with the knee slightly bent, raise the right leg, with the knee bent and the foot crooked. At the same time, both arms circle downward and inward, crossing in front of the abdomen with the hands changed into fists and the right one below.

(222)

The right leg kicks forcibly to the lower-right with the toes pointing forward and the sole approximately 30 cm above the floor, force concentrated on the heel. Meanwhile, swing both arms respectively outward with the fists explosively vibrating, force concentrated on the back of the fists. Look in the direction of the right foot.

Purpose: If the opponent thrusts his right fist into your belly or ribs, you can turn sideways, protecting yourself by hooking his arm with your right arm. Then, you can kick him on the knee or on the lower leg with your right foot, and strike to the belly or on the ribs with your right fist.

60

Form 21
Punch with Body Draped Over —
Right and Left

(223 - 224)

Lower the right foot onto the floor. Turn your torso to the left with the weight predominantly kept on the left leg to form a left bow stance. At the same time, the left fist withdraws to the left side of the waist with the centre of the fist facing upward; while the right fist swings downward, leftward and forward to the chest level with the back of the fist on top. The left fist then swings forward and upward to the nose level.

(225 - 226)

Turn your torso to the right and shift your weight

onto the right leg to form a right bow stance. Along with the turn of the torso, the left fist circles rightward to the front of the chest with the arm bent and the centre of the fist facing backward; while the right fist swings upward, rightward and then withdraws to the right side of the waist with the centre of the fist facing upward.

(227 - 231)

Turn your torso to the left and shift your weight onto the left leg to form a left bow stance. At the same time, the left fist continues to circle rightward, downward and leftward until it gets to the left side of the waist with the centre of the fist facing upward; while the right fist moves sideways up with the arm rotating inward, and then swings to the left at nose level with the elbow

61

bent and the forearm rotating outward, the centre of the fist facing backward.

Purpose (take the right form as an example): When the opponent nestles up from behind and makes a surprise attack, you can turn to the right swiftly, butting your right elbow against his chest and then thrusting your right fist into his belly.

Form 22
Lean with Back Twisted

(232 - 233)
Turn your torso slightly to the right, then back to the left. Along with the twist of the torso, the right forearm rotates inward and revolves on the elbow leftward, downward and rightward. Correspondingly, the right fist wheels on the wrist

counterclockwise.

(234 - 235)
Turn your torso to the right and shift your weight onto the right leg to form a right bow stance. On leaning rightward and backward explosively, raise the right arm to the upper-right with the elbow bent, the fist about 10 cm apart from the forehead, the eye of the fist down and the centre of the fist facing outward. Meanwhile, the left

forearm rotates inward so as to turn the centre of the left fist down and place the forefist against the left side of the waist. Throw the left shoulder and the left elbow slightly onward in the meantime. Look to the lower-left.

Purpose: When the opponent pulls your arm so you happen to get close to him, or when you do it on your own initiative, you can twist your

torso to invalidate his control and strike him by leaning forcibly against his chest with your shoulder and back.

Another method can be described as follows: If the opponent thrusts his right fist into your chest, you can turn rightward to dodge the blow. You can also break his arm by dragging his wrist to the right with your right hand and butting your left shoulder and arm against his elbow.

Form 23
Blue Dragon Goes Out of Water

(236 - 237)

Turn your torso to the left and shift your weight onto the left leg. Meanwhile, rotate the right forearm outward and swing the right fist to the front at head level with the centre of the fist

facing backward.

(238 - 240)

Turn your torso to the right and shift your weight onto the right leg. At the same time, the right fist continues to swing leftward, downward, and then withdraws to the side of the right ribs with the centre of the fist facing upward. Simultaneously, with the forearm rotating outward, the

left fist swings downward, sideways up, and then rightward, until it gets to the front-left at a level slightly higher than the shoulder, the centre of the fist facing upward. Eyes follow the left fist.

(241-243)

Turn your torso to the left and shift your weight onto the left leg. At the same time, the right fist drops with the forearm rotating inward, then

63

swings sideways up and to the front-right at nose level with the forearm rotating outward, the centre of the fist facing backward; while the left fist continues to circle rightward, downward and leftward to the left side of the waist with the centre of the fist facing upward.

Purpose: When the opponent thrusts his left fist into your belly, you can swing your right arm downward to deflect the blow. Then, you can punch to the crotch or the belly with your left hand and right fist in quick succession.

(244)

As you turn your torso to the right and shift your weight to the right, the right fist drops and withdraws to the front of the abdomen with the forearm rotating inward so that the centre of the fist nestles gently against the abdomen. At the same time, the left hand, with the forearm rotating inward, the thumb and the forefingers straightened and separated, and the other three together rolled up in the hollow of the hand, springs explosively to the lower-front-right at abdomen level, the palm facing obliquely downward.

(245 - 247)

Turn your torso swiftly to the left and shift your weight onto the left leg to form a left-dominated horse-riding stance. Along with the turn of the torso, with the forearm rotating inward, the right fist springs swiftly and explosively to the lower-front-right about 20 cm apart from the right knee, the centre of the fist facing obliquely downward, force concentrated on the back of the fist. Meanwhile, the left hand withdraws rapidly until the palm nestles to the left part of the abdomen.

Form 24
White Ape Presents Fruit

(248 - 252)

Turn your torso slightly to the left before twisting it back to the right. Shift your weight to the left and then back to the right. At the same time, the right fist swings downward, leftward and up-ward until it gets to the front of the chest with the elbow bent; while the left hand, still gently clinging to the abdomen, revolves on the wrist downward, leftward and upward, drawing a small circle with the forearm rotating inward. Throw the left shoulder slightly onward in the mean-time. Eyes follow the right fist.

(253 - 258)

Turn your torso to the left with the toes of the left foot turned outward and shift your weight completely onto the left leg. As you straighten the left leg naturally to stand up, raise the right leg to abdomen level with the knee bent and the foot suspended. At the same time, the right fist continues to circle upward, rightward, downward, and then swings forward and upward passing beside the hip to the upper-front at nose level, the centre of the fist facing the upper-rear; while the left hand clenches into a fist and moves to the left side of the waist with the centre of the fist facing upward. Eyes follow the right fist.

Purpose: When the opponent launches an attack on your left ribs or belly with his right hand, you can press his arm with your left arm to

65

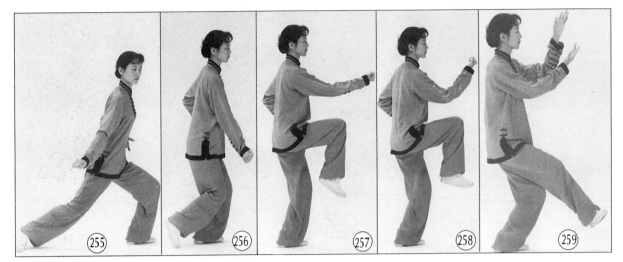

deflect the blow. You can also raise the right knee to strike the crotch and swing the right fist to punch him on the chin or on the face.

Form 25
Six Sealings and Four Closings — Left

(259 - 261)
Bend the left leg to squat down and lower the right foot onto the floor in front with the toes turned out. As the torso twists slightly to the

right, open both your fists. At the same time, with the forearm rotating inward, the left hand stretches from above the right arm to the upper-front at nose level, the palm facing obliquely downward and fingers pointing to the upper-front; while the right hand drops beneath the left elbow with the palm facing the upper-rear.

(262 - 264)
Shift your weight onto the right leg. The left foot takes a step forward with the toes turned slightly inward. As your torso turns to the right, the right hand moves slightly downward and then rises again to the front of the right shoulder, with the middle finger, the ring finger and the little finger rolling inward and upward. Meanwhile, the left hand circles downward, rightward, forward and

66

upward to the front at shoulder level with the palm facing upward and the fingers pointing to the front-left.

(265 - 266)

The left foot goes a little further. Turn your torso slightly to the right and shift your weight slightly leftward. At the same time, with the arms bent, both hands revolve on the wrists outward and

backward until the hands get to the upper-front of the shoulders respectively, the palms facing the upper-front and the fingers pointing to the upper-rear. Look to the front-right.

(267 - 269)

Shift your weight completely onto the left leg. Bring the right foot forward with the ball scraping along the floor and then place it next to the left

one to form a right empty stance. As the torso turns to the left, both hands press forward and downward, passing beside the cheeks, to the lower-front-left at abdomen level with the palms facing each other obliquely. Set your eyes on the hands.

Purpose: When the opponent thrusts both hands into your chest, you can part the arms in

the middle with both your hands. Then, you can step up with your left foot and punch him in the chest or in the belly with both your palms.

Form 26
Single Whip — Right

(270 - 271)

As your torso turns slightly to the left, the left hand withdraws to the left side of the waist with

the palm tuned up; while the right hand pushes forward from above the left one with the palm facing the lower-front. Set your eyes on the right hand.

(272 - 274)

As your torso turns slightly to the right, the right hand withdraws to the front of the abdomen with the forearm rotating outward so as to turn the palm up, the fingers pointing to the left. Simultaneously, with the fingertips brought together and the wrist crooked to form a hook, the left hand stretches from above the right palm to the upper-left at shoulder level, the tip of the hook pointing to the right. Look in the direction of the left hook.

(275 - 276)

Squat down a little more on the left leg. Lift the

right foot and move it to the right side with the heel scraping along the floor until it is three and a half foot lengths from the left one.

(277 - 278)

Set the right foot firm on the floor. Turn your torso to the right and shift your weight to the right leg with the toes of the left foot turned slightly inward.

(279 - 281)

Turn your torso to the left and shift your weight onto the left leg again. Simultaneously, the right hand stretches toward the upper-left with the palm facing upward and the fingers pointing to the front-left.

68

(282 - 283)

When the right hand gets close to the left elbow, rotate the forearm inward to turn the palm out.

(284 - 286)

Turn your torso to the right and shift your weight onto the right leg to form a right-dominated horse-riding stance. Meanwhile, the right hand moves in a horizontal arc to the front-right, forming a standing palm with the wrist sunk, the elbow dropped, the shoulder lowered and the waist relaxed. Eyes follow the right hand.

Purpose: The same as those described in Figures 160-172, only reversing "left" and "right".

69

Stage Four
Form 27
Double Stamps with Feet

(287 - 291)
Turn your torso to the left and shift your weight
to the left leg with the toes of the right foot turned

inward. At the same time, the right hand circles
downward and leftward; while the left hook
returns to a palm with the forearm rotating inward to turn the palm out.

(292 - 296)

Turn your torso to the right and shift your weight on to the right leg with the toes of the right foot turned outward. At the same time, the right hand rises with the forearm rotating inward to turn the palm out, then moves in a horizontal arc to the front-right at a level slightly higher than the shoulder; while the left hand moves downward and rightward with the forearm rotating outward.

(297)

Shift your weight completely onto the right leg and bring the left foot next to and about 10 cm apart from the right one. At the same time, the right hand continues to circle rightward and downward; while the left hand moves to the right past the abdomen.

(298 - 299)
Turn your torso slightly to the right and shift your weight completely onto the left leg. Move the right foot half a step forward with the ball lightly resting on the floor. At the same time, the right hand moves slightly to the left and then rises to the front at chest level with the forearm rotating outward to turn the palm up, the fingers pointing forward; while the left hand continues to rise until it gets close to the inner side of the right forearm with the palm facing upward.

(300)
Bend the left leg to squat down a little more with the whole sole of the right foot lightly resting on the floor. Meanwhile, both hands press slightly downward and forward with the forearm rotating inward to turn the palms down.

(301)
While the right leg swings up with the knee bent, the left leg stamps the floor to jump into the air. Meanwhile, hold both hands up to the shoulder level with the arms rotating outward to turn the palms up.

(302 - 305)
On landing, the left foot and the right foot stamp the floor with a smack in sequence. Simultaneously, both hands press down to the chest level with the arms rotating inward to turn the palms down, the fingers pointing to the front.

Purpose: When the opponent thrusts his left hand into your chest, you can grasp him by the wrist and the elbow with your left hand and your right hand, pressing the arm from both sides.

Then, you can hold his arm up and tread on his foot. The moment he is attempting to withdraw, you can either twist his arm and push it forward and downward explosively or punch him in the chest with both your palms, thus forcing him to tumble.

Form 28
Jade Girl Works at Shuttles

(306 - 307)
The right foot takes half a step forward. As you shift your weight onto the right leg, the right hand thrusts straight ahead at throat level; while the left hand slightly withdraws. Keep both palms down with the fingers pointing forward.

(308 - 309)
As the left leg swings for- ward

, the right leg stamps on the floor to leap forward. In the meantime, the left hand thrusts, from above the right palm, to the front at shoulder level; while the right hand withdraws beneath the left elbow with the fingers pointing to the left.

(310 - 311)
Turn your torso about 90 degrees to the right before the left foot lands on the floor. The right

foot then takes a step to the left behind the left leg, with the weight predominantly kept on the left leg to form a right back-cross stance. Simultaneously, the right hand moves to the front of the abdomen with the fingers pointing to the left. The left arm remains on the left side.

(312 - 313)
Turn your torso about 180 degrees to the right

73

and shift your weight slightly rightward with the toes of the left foot turned inward. Along with the turn of the torso, the right hand circles round until it gets to the front of the right shoulder and a little higher than the shoulder level, with the arm slightly bent and the palm turned out. The left arm remains on the left side.

(314 - 315)

Turn your torso to the left and shift your weight onto the left leg. The right foot first moves toward the left one, then goes sideways again with the knee turned inward. In the meantime, the right hand continues to circle rightward, downward and leftward, passing before the abdomen with the palm facing the left; while the left hand moves upward and rightward to the

front of the chest with the palm facing the right.

(316 - 323)

Turn your torso to the right and shift your weight slightly to the right leg to form a right-dominated horse-riding stance. At the same time, the right hand continues to circle leftward, upward and then rightward, until it goes to the front-right at a level slightly higher than the shoulder with the

elbow dropped and the palm turned out; while the left hand moves slightly to the right, then drops from inside the right arm to the front of the abdomen with the arm bent and the palm facing upward. Eyes follow the right hand.

Purpose: Thrust your palms straight into the opponent's throat successively.

74

Form 29
Beast's Head Pose

(324 - 327)

Twist your torso slightly to the left before turning the torso back to the right and shifting the weight onto the right leg again. At the same time, the right hand circles downward and leftward to the

75

front of the abdomen with the palm facing the left and the fingers pointing to the front; while the left hand rises to the front of the chest with the elbow and the wrist bent, the palm facing the left and the fingers pointing downward. Eyes follow the right hand.

(328 - 330)

As you turn your torso slightly to the left and shift your weight slightly to the left, clench both fists. The right fist rises from inside the left forearm to the front of the chest; while the left fist moves forward and downward round the right forearm to the front of the abdomen beneath the right arm. Keep the centre of both fists backward with the eyes of the fists on top.

76

(331)
Shift your weight slightly onto the right leg to form a right-dominated horse-riding stance. At the same time, the right fist comes to the front at shoulder level with the elbow dropped, the forearm tilted in front of the chest; while the left fist pauses close to the inner side of the right elbow with the forearm crosswise in front of the chest. The centres of the fists remain backward with the eyes of the fists on top. Keep both arms well rounded. Set your eyes on the right fist.

Purpose: When the opponent grasps you by your right wrist, you can withdraw your arm backward and downward to lead his hand. Then, you can bend his arm backward by lifting your right hand and pressing his elbow with your left arm. The moment he is attempting to extricate

himself from such an awkward predicament, you can step up immediately to punch him in the chest or on the nose with the back of your right fist.

Form 30
Dragon on the Ground

(332 - 333)
While twisting your torso slightly to the left and shifting your weight slightly to the left, open both your fists with the wrists relaxed.

(334 - 335)
Turn your torso to the right and shift your weight onto the right leg to form a right bow stance. At the same time, the right hand moves leftward,

upward, then rightward to the front-right at about eyebrow level with the arm well rounded, the palm facing outward and the fingers pointing to the front-left; while the left hand moves downward, leftward, upward and then rightward, drawing a small circle with the wrist revolving round, until it reach the front-right beneath the right arm, with the palm facing outward and the fingers pointing to the upper-front-left. Set your eyes on the left hand.

(336)
Squat down a little more with the toes of the left foot turned outward and those of the right one inward. The left arm drops in the meantime.

(337 - 342)
Turn your torso to the left and shift your weight

onto the left leg to form a left bow stance. At the same time, the left hand continues to circle leftward, forward and upward with the forearm rotating outward, until it gets to the front at nose level with the palm facing obliquely upward. Simultaneously, the right hand drops and then moves passing beside the right hip to the front at about chest level with the palm facing the left.

(343)
Clench both your fists. Bend the left arm and swing the right fist upward.

(344 - 346)
Turn your torso to the right and shift your weight onto the right leg. Then, bend the right leg to squat down and stretch the left leg sideways to form a left crouch stance. Along with the turn of the torso, the right fist moves upward and rightward to the upper-right at eyebrow level with the arm bent and the forearm rotating inward; while the left fist drops inside the right arm past the abdomen. Then, as the torso turns slightly to the left, the left fist continues to stretch along the inner side of the left leg to the front. Eyes follow the left fist.

Purpose: When the opponent thrusts his right fist into your chest, you can grasp him by the wrist with your right hand and pull his arm toward the upper-right. Then, you can squat down and insert your left leg behind the opponent to lock his foot, and stretch your left arm under his crotch to throw him to the ground.

Form 31
Step Forward with Seven Stars

(347 - 349)
Turn your torso to the left with the toes of the left foot slightly turned outward. Straighten the right leg and shift the weight forward so as to form a right bow stance. At the same time, the left fist

continues to move forward and upward to the front at chin level; while the right fist drops to the side of the right hip. Eyes follow the left fist.

(350 - 353)

Shift your weight completely onto the left leg. With the ball scraping along the floor, bring the right foot a step forward and place the toes gently on the floor in front to form a right empty stance.

Meanwhile, as the left fist moves slightly inward with the forearm rotating outward, the right fist continues to swing forward and upward, so that both wrists cross in front of the chest with the centres of both fists facing backward.

(354 - 356)

With the forearms remaining crossed and rotating inward, both fists revolve round the intersection of the wrists backward, downward, forward and upward, drawing a small circle before the fists change to palms. Both hands then push slightly forward with the palms facing outward. Look in the direction of the hands.

(357 - 360)
With the forearm remaining crossed and rotating outward, both hands revolve round the intersection of the wrists forward, downward, backward and upward, drawing a small circle before the hands clench to make fists again. The centres of both fists face backward.

Purpose: If the opponent seizes your wrists conversely with both hands, you can bend your arms and cross the fists, and revolve the fists to loosen the grip. Then, with the fists changed to palms, you can punch him explosively in the chest with both your palms.

Form 32
Step Back and Mount the Tiger

(361 - 363)
As the right foot takes a step to the rear-right, open both fists with both forearms rotating inward so as to turn the palms obliquely outward.

(364 - 367)

As your torso turns to the right, set the right foot firm on the floor and shift your weight to the right. At the same time, lower both hands with the palms turned down, and then separate them. Each hand moves to the side above the knee with the palm facing obliquely downward.

(368 - 374)

Shift your weight onto the right leg and bring the left foot next to the right one with the ball resting on the floor. At the same time, the right hand continues to circle sideways up and then, with the arm bent, moves leftward to the front at head level, the palm facing the left, the fingers pointing upward; while the left hand circles leftward, upward, to the right and downward until it gets to the front of the abdomen beneath the right elbow with the palm facing the right and the fingers pointing obliquely upward. Set your eyes on the right hand.

Purpose: If the opponent kicks you on the right leg or in the crotch, you can move your right leg back and turn your torso to the right, and swing the left hand outward to protect the knee. Thus, the attack is bound to come to nothing.

82

(371) (372) (373) (374) (375) (376)

Form 33
Turn Round and Swing Lotus

(375 - 376)

Set the left foot firm on the floor and shift the weight slightly onto the left leg with the toes of the right foot turned outward. Then, shift your weight completely onto the right leg, and lift the left leg upward and rightward with the knee bent.

At the same time, the right hand revolves on the wrist leftward, downward and rightward with the forearm rotating inward, thus turning the palm out with the fingers pointing to the left; while the left hand moves to the side of the left hip with the palm facing downward.

(377 - 378)

As the torso turns to the right, the left

(377) (378) (379) (379') (380)

foot lands to the front-right with the toes turned inward.

(379 - 381)

As your torso continues to turn round to the right, shift your weight onto the left leg. Both hands simultaneously move round until the right hand gets to the right side and the left hand to the rightward of the chest with palms turned down.

The right leg then swings toward the upper-left and sweeps across the face to the right in a fan-shaped arc. Meanwhile, both hands wave leftward, slapping the outer side of the instep of the right foot in succession in front of the face (left palm first, then right palm). Set your eyes on the right foot.

Purpose: If the opponent launches an attack on your left leg, you can raise the left leg and turn

(381) (382) (383) (384)

around to the right to dodge the blow. Then, on landing forward with the left foot, you can swing your right leg to strike him in the waist or the ribs.

Form 34
The Head-on Cannon

(382 - 384)
As the torso continues to turn to the right, lower

the right foot and place it to the rear-right on the floor. Meanwhile, both arms move to the front-left at chest level with the palms facing the lower-left. Look in the direction of the right hand.

(385)
Turn your torso to the right and shift your weight to the right with the toes of the left foot turned inward. Following the turn of the   torso,

(385) (386) (387)

both hands move horizontally to the right, with the left hand at chest level and the right hand at a level slightly higher than the shoulder. Rotate the left forearm slightly outward and the right one slightly inward so as to turn the palms outward while they are moving. Eyes follow the right hand.

(386 - 390)
Turn your torso slightly to the left and shift your weight onto the left leg. At the same time, both hands continue to circle rightward, downward and leftward with the right forearm rotating outward and the left one inward before they are changed into fists. The left fist then withdraws to the left side of the waist; while the right fist gets to the front of the abdomen. Keep both arms bent

84

and the eyes of the fists on top. Eyes follow the right fist.

(391)

Turn your torso to the right and shift your weight onto the right leg to form a right bow stance. Simultaneously, both fists together punch to the front-right with the right forearm crosswise in front of the chest and the left fist about 10 cm behind the right wrist. Keep the centres of the fists backward with the eyes of the fists on top. Concentrate force on the backs of the fists.

Purpose: If the opponent launches an attack with his right hand, you can grasp his arm with both hands and pull it to the lower-left. Immediately after that, you can clench your fists and punch the chest or the belly with your right forearm and fist. You should straighten the left leg and turn the torso to the right swiftly to exert force, and push the left fist forward to assist the strike.

Form 35
Buddha's Warrior Attendant Pounds with a Pestle and Mortar — Left

(392 - 393)

Open both the fists with the wrists relaxed. Accom-panied be a small twist of the torso, both hands revolve on the wrists leftward, upward and rightward, drawing a small circle respectively with the left forearm rotating inward and the right one outward, so as to turn the palms outward with the fingers pointing to the right. Then, as you turn your torso to the left and shift your weight onto the left leg, both hands move horizontally round to the left. Eyes follow the right hand.

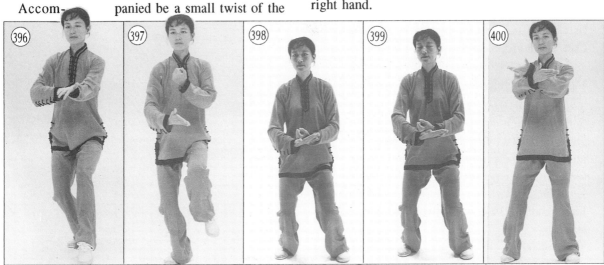

(394 - 396)

Turn your torso to the right and shift your weight completely onto the right leg with the toes of the right foot turned slightly outward . The left foot then takes a step forward, with the ball first scraping along the floor and then resting gently on the floor, to form a left empty stance. At the same time, the left hand continues to swing leftward, downward and forward to the front of the left hip with the palm facing the upper-front; while the right hand moves downward, forward, upward and backward, drawing a vertical circle before it lies crosswise on the left forearm with the elbow bent and the palm facing obliquely backward. Set your eyes on the left hand.

86

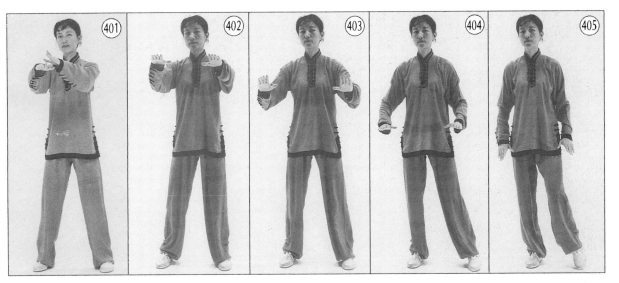

(397)

As you straighten the right leg slightly, raise the left leg with the knee bent and the foot naturally suspended. At the same time, the right hand drops to the front of the abdomen with the palm facing upward and the fingers pointing to the left; while the left hand clenches to make a fist and comes up to chest level with the centre of the fist facing upward. Set your eyes on the left fist.

(398 - 399)

Without any pause, as you bend the right leg slightly to squat down, the left foot stamps on the floor forcibly with the foot parallel to and about 20 cm apart from the right one. Meanwhile, the left fist smashes down into the right palm with the centre of the fist remaining upward.

Purpose: The same as those described in Figures 10-18, only reversing "left" and "right".

Form 36
Closing Form

(400)

Place your weight evenly on both legs. As the legs are gradually straightened, raise both arms and cross the wrists in front of the chest with the left fist opened and the palms facing upward.

(401)

Stand erect. Rotate both arms inward so as to turn the palms down. Look forward.

(402 - 405)

Separate your hands about a shoulder-width apart with the fingers pointing forward. Then, lower them slowly and naturally to the sides of the hips.

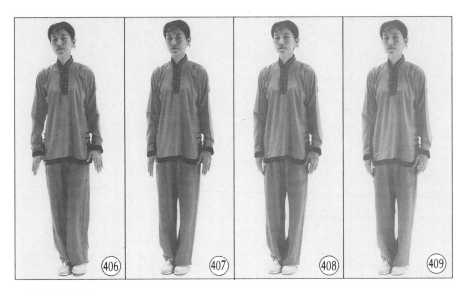

(406 - 409)
Shift your weight onto the right leg and bring the
left foot next to the right one to stand naturally
with the feet together and the weight evenly
placed on both legs. Look straight ahead.

Part 2
Chen style
Fifty-six Movements
Taijiquan

(Competition Routine)

1. The Names of the Fifty-six Movements

Stage One
1. Opening Form
2. Buddha's Warrior Attendant Pounds with a Pestle and Mortar — Right
3. Clasp and Tie the Coat
4. Six Sealings and Four Closings — Right
5. Single Whip — Left
6. Deflect, Parry and Punch
7. Heart-protecting Punch
8. White Crane Spreads Wings
9. Walk Obliquely and Twist Step
10. Lift and Retract
11. Wade Forward
12. Cover Hand and Thrust Fist — Right
13. Punch with Body Draped Over
14. Lean with Back Twisted
15. Blue Dragon Goes Out of Water
16. Slice with Hand
17. Turn Flowers Out and Wave Sleeves
18. Turn Flowers Out from Sea Bottom
19. Cover Hand and Thrust Fist — Left
20. Six sealings and Four Closings — Left
21. Single Whip — Right

Stage Two
22. Wave Hands like Clouds — Right
23. Wave Hands like Clouds — Left
24. High Pat on Horse
25. Bombardments in Series — Right
26. Bombardments in Series — Left
27. Flash the Back

Stage Three
28. Punch toward the Crotch
29. White Ape Presents Fruit

30. Push with Both Hands
31. Mid-level Skill
32. The Former Trick
33. The Latter Trick
34. Part the Wild Horse's Mane — Right
35. Part the Wild Horse's Mane — Left
36. Swing Lotus and Drop into Splits
37. Golden Cock Stands on Single Leg — Left and Right

Stage Four
38. Step Back and Roll Arms
39. Step Back and Press Elbow
40. Rub Instep
41. Kick Sideward with Right Foot
42. Turn Flowers Out from Sea Bottom
43. Punch toward the Ground
44. Turnover and Jump Slap Kick
45. Double Stamps with Feet
46. Kick with Right Heel
47. Jade Girl Works at Shuttles
48. Smooth Elbow Butt
49. Wrapping Firecrackers
50. Dragon on the Ground
51. Step Forward with Seven Stars
52. Step Back and Mount the Tiger
53. Turn Round and Swing Lotus
54. The Head-on Cannon
55. Buddha's Warrior Attendant Pounds with a Pestle and Mortar — Left
56. Closing Form

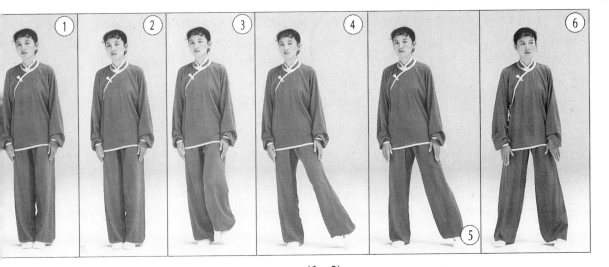

2. Performance of the Fifty-six Movements

Stage One
Form 1
Opening Form

(1 - 2)
Stand upright naturally with the feet together, the arms hanging down and the hands gently clinging to the sides of thighs. Hold your head erect, chin slightly in, chest and abdomen relaxed. Concentrate your attention and breathe naturally. Look horizontally foreword.

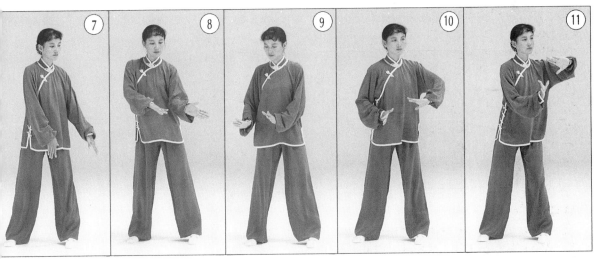

(3 - 6)
Shift your weight naturally onto the right leg. Raise the left foot gently and move it to the left about a shoulder-width apart from and parallel to the right one with the tiptoes of the feet pointing forward. Then, distribute your weight evenly on both feet.

Form 2
Buddha's Warrior Attendant Pounds with a Pestle and Mortar — Right

(7 - 9)
Shift your weight slightly leftward. Turn your torso slightly to the left and then back to the right.

91

In coordination with the twist of the body, swing both your arms clockwise in front of the abdomen so that both hands respectively sway in a small horizontal circle from the left to the right side of the body using wrists as axes, the palms turned down.

(10 - 11)
Turn your torso slightly to the left and raise both arms to the front-left at shoulder level with the elbows slightly bent.

(12 - 13)
Bend the legs slightly and shift your weight onto the left leg, with the toes of the right foot turning about 90 degrees out using the heel as the pivot. Meanwhile, rotate the left arm outward and the right one inward so as to turn both palms out with

the fingers pointing to the left.

(14 - 16)
Shift your weight completely onto the right leg and turn your torso to the right. At the same time, both hands move in a horizontal arc to the front-right. Then, raise the left leg with the knee bent.

(17)
As you bend the right leg to squat yourself down a little more, the left foot shovels to the front-left with the toes tilted up and the inner side of the heel scraping along the floor. Simultaneously, push both hands further to the right with the palms still facing outward. Look in the direction of the right hand.

92

(18)

As you begin to shift your weight leftward, both hands respectively revolve clockwise round their own wrists so as to turn the palms down.

(19 - 21)

As you turn your torso to the left, place the sole of the left foot fully on the floor and shift your weight toward the left leg. At the same time, the left hand drops, then moves forward and upward until it gets to the front of the chest with the elbow bent; while the right hand swings downward.

(22 - 23)

Shift your weight completely onto the left leg. The right leg then takes a step forward with the toes gently resting on the floor to form a right empty stance. At the same time, the right hand continues to swing, passing beside the right knee, to the front-right of the abdomen with the palm obliquely facing upward and the fingers pointing to the lower-front; while the left hand withdraws, resting itself crosswise upon the right

forearm with the palm facing downward.

(24 - 25)

Raise the right leg with the knee bent. At the same time, the left hand drops to the front of the abdomen with the palm facing upward; while the right hand changes into a fist and rises to nose level with the centre of the fist facing backward.

(26)

As the right foot forcibly stamps on the floor about 20 cm apart from the left one, the right fist smashes down into the left palm with the centre of the fist facing upward.

Form 3
Clasp and Tie the Coat

(27 - 28)

As you turn your torso slightly to the left, the left hand, holding the right fist in the hollow of the

palm, moves leftward and upward until it gets to the front of the left shoulder. Then, turn your torso slightly to the right and cross your arms in front of the chest with the right arm in and the fist changed back to a palm.

(29 - 32)

Turn your torso to the right with your weight predominantly on the right leg. Then, shift your weight completely onto the left leg and raise the right leg with the knee bent. At the same time, rotate both arms inward so as to turn the palms out. The right hand circles upward, to the right, downward and then leftward; while the left hand swings downward, leftward, upward and then rightward. Both arms thus cross in front of the chest with the right one out and both palms obliquely facing upward.

(33 - 34)

As you bend the left leg to squat yourself down a little more, the right foot shovels to the right with the inner side of the heel scraping along the floor.

(35 - 38)

Turn your torso slightly to the left and then back to the right, and shift your weight rightward to form a right-dominated horse-riding stance (with both legs bent to take a half squat, keeping the weight predominantly on the right leg). At the same time, rotate the right forearm inward to turn the palm out. The right hand rises a little and then moves in a horizontal arc, passing before the chin, to the front-right at shoulder level, forming a standing palm with the wrist sunk, the hollow of the hand obliquely facing forward; while the left hand drops to the front of the abdomen with the palm facing upward. Look in the direction of the right hand.

Form 4
Six Sealings and Four Closings — Right

(39 - 41)

Turn your torso slightly to the left and shift your weight slightly leftward before turning the torso swiftly back to the right and shifting the weight rightward. In coordination with the twist of the body, with the forearm rotating first inward and then outward, the right hand revolves downward, backward and upward, using the wrist as the axis, thus drawing a small vertical circle until it gets to the front-right again. In the meantime, with the wrist crooked, the forearm rotating first inward then outward, the left hand revolves round the wrist, drawing a small complete circle

clockwise with the back of the hand gently against the abdomen, until it resumes the previous position with the palm facing upward.

(42 - 45)

As you turn your torso slightly to the left and shift your weight slightly leftward, the right hand pulls downward and leftward, then rises to the front-left of the chest with the elbow bent and the palm facing the rear-left. At the same time, rotate the left forearm inward and crook the hand down at the wrist. The left hand thus comes up with the palm facing the left and the thumb side of the hand gently scraping along the left ribs. The left hand then gets close to the right wrist. Without any pause, as you turn your torso to the right and shift your weight to the right, both hands push to the front-right at shoulder level with the palms

facing backward. Both hands then stretch further out, with the right forearm rotating inward and the left forearm slightly outward so as to turn the right palm out and the left one obliquely up. Eyes follow the right hand.

(46 - 47)
As you turn your torso slightly to the left and shift your weight leftward, the right hand moves downward, leftward and then upward, drawing a small vertical circle until it comes to the front-right again at a level slightly lower than the shoulder, the palm facing upward, the fingers pointing to the right and the elbow bent. Meanwhile, the left hand drops, and then rises to the upper-left beside the left ear with the elbow bent and the wrist crooked. The little finger, ring finger and middle finger successively move in

during the motion with the fingertips pointing obliquely to the ground. Look in the direction of the right palm.

(48 - 50)
Turn your torso to the left. Rotate both forearms inward to turn the palms up. Both hands simultaneously sway outward and backward until they respectively get close to the ears above the shoulders with the elbows bent.

(51 - 56)

Turn your torso to the right and shift your weight onto the right leg. Bring the left foot to about 20 cm beside the right one with the toes resting on the floor, the knee bent and turned out. Along with the turn of the body, both hands press from above the shoulders to the lower-right beside the right hip, with the palms obliquely facing downward, the thumb and forefinger sides of the

hands in opposition to each other. Look in the direction between the palms.

Form 5
Single Whip — Left

(57 - 58)
Immediately after you turn your torso slightly to the left, turn it back to the right. In coordination with the small and swift twist of the torso, the right hand withdraws to the inner side of the left forearm with the palm turned up and the elbow bent; while the left hand pushes further to the front-right from above the right palm, with the hollow of the hand turned down.

(59 - 60)
As you turn your torso to the left, the left hand withdraws to the front of the abdomen with the elbow bent and the arm rotated outward to turn

the palm up; while the right hand changes into a hook with the wrist crooked and the fingertips together and down, and reaches from above the left palm to the upper-front-right at shoulder level. Look in the direction of the right hand. Then, shift your weight completely onto the right leg and raise the left leg with the knee bent.

(61 - 62)
As you bend the right leg to squat yourself down, the left foot shovels to the left with the inner side of the heel scraping along the floor. Set your eyes on the left foot.

(63)
As you turn your torso slightly to the left, place the sole of the left foot fully on the floor and bend

98

the left leg at the knee to shift your weight leftward.

(64 - 66)

Without any pause, turn your torso to the right and shift your weight rightward. Meanwhile, the left hand stretches before the abdomen to the front of the right shoulder.

(67 - 70)

Rotate the left arm inward to turn the palm out. Then, turn your torso to the left and shift your weight leftward to form a left-dominated horse-riding stance. Meanwhile, the left hand moves in a horizontal arc, passing before the chest, to the front-left at a level slightly lower than the shoulder, forming a standing palm with the elbow dropped, the wrist sunk and the hollow of the hand obliquely facing forward. Look in the direction of the left hand.

Points for Attention: In this movement, the roll of the hands, as well as the rise of the right hooked hand, should harmonize with the twist of the torso. You should also manifest a style of strength as though twining silk thread or drawing it from a cocoon. Moreover, you ought to keep your buttocks in, hips lowered, waist and shoul-

ders relaxed, and direct your energy stream down in the fixed position.

Form 6
Deflect, Parry and Punch

(71 - 72)
As you turn your torso slightly to the left, both

hands, with the right one changed back to a palm, sway respectively round their own wrists, drawing a small circle counterclockwise.

(73 - 74)
Turn your torso to the right and shift your weight rightward. Meanwhile, clench both your fists. The fists then move downward and rightward to the lower-right beside the right hip, with the

centre of the right fist up and that of the left one down. Look in the direction between the fists.

(75 - 77)
Turn your torso promptly to the left and shift your weight slightly leftward to form a half squat with both legs bent. At the same time, with the left arm rotating outward to turn the centre of the fist up and the right arm inward to turn that of the right fist down, both fists swing explosively in a horizontal arc, passing before the chest to the left side, force concentrated on the eyes of the fists.

100

Look in the direction of the left fist.

(78 - 79)

Turn your torso slightly to the right and then back to the left. Along with the twist of the torso, both fists sway upward, rightward, downward and leftward, drawing a small circle clockwise, until they get to the left side again. Rotate the left arm inward and the right arm outward so as to turn the centre of the left fist down and that of the right one up in the meantime.

(80 - 81)

As you turn your torso promptly to the right and shift your weight slightly to the right, both fists swing explosively in a horizontal arc, passing before the chest to the right side, force concentrated on the eyes of the fists. Look in the direction of the right fist.

Form 7
Heart-protecting Punch

(82 - 83)

Turn your torso further to the right and shift your weight rightward. Meanwhile, with the arms rotating inward, both fists drop to the lower-right outside the right knee. Look in the direction between the fists.

(84 - 86)

Shift your weight completely onto the right leg and raise the left leg with the knee bent. As you turn round to the left, the right leg drives the floor hard so as to jump up. After the left foot lands, the right leg takes a step forward, keeping the weight predominantly on the left leg. Along with the

turn and the jump of the body, the left fist swings upward, passing before the forehead, then drops to the left side of the waist; while the right fist follows up, and then swings to the front. Without any pause, the left fist continues to move sideways up; while the right fist drops to the front of the abdomen.

(87 - 88)

As you turn your torso slightly to the right and shift your weight forward, the left fist continues to move rightward and then drops to the front of the right ribs with the elbow bent and the forearm crosswise in front of the chest; while the right fist, with the elbow bent, rises from inside the left forearm and then reaches out to the front-left at chest level. Keep the centres of the fists back-

ward and look in the direction of the right fist.

(89)

As you turn your torso slightly to the left and squat yourself down a little more to form a right-dominated horse-riding stance, round both your arms, applying a warding-off force forward. You ought to get the sense of holding the back of your torso firmly backward throughout this motion.

Form 8
White Crane Spreads Wings

(90 - 92)

As you turn your torso to the right and shift your weight completely onto the right leg with the toes of the foot turned out, raise the left foot with the knee slightly bent, and bring it forward. At the

same time, open both your fists. The right hand stretches to the front of the left shoulder with the palm obliquely facing downward; while the left hand reaches to the side of the right hip with the palm obliquely facing upward. Look in the direction of the left palm.

(93)

The left foot shovels to the front-left with the

inner side of the heel scraping along the floor. At the same time, rotate both your arms inward to turn the palms out. The right hand moves downward and the left one upward, thus crossing the arms in front of the chest with the left one out.

(94 - 96)

Turn your torso to the left and shift your weight onto the left leg with the sole of the foot placed

fully on the floor. Then, bring the right foot forward and place the ball on the floor about 20 cm to the side of the left heel. At the same time, the left hand expands upward and leftward, passing before the face, to the front-left at a level slightly higher than the head, with the palm facing outward and the fingers pointing to the upper-right; while the right hand drops, passing before the abdomen, to the side of the right hip, with the palm facing downward and the fingers pointing to the front-left. Keep both arms well rounded in the fixed position. Look straight ahead.

Form 9
Walk Obliquely and Twist Step

(97 - 100)

Turn your torso slightly to the right and then back to the left with the right foot twisting on its toes. Following the twist of the torso, the left hand swings rightward, downward and then leftward to the side of the left hip with the palm turned down; while the right hand rises from the side, and then moves to the upper-front-right with the palm turned out.

(101 - 104)

As you turn your torso slightly to the right, the right foot rises and then stamps on the floor with the knee bent. Coinciding with the landing of the right foot, the left foot comes up with the knee bent, and then shovels to the left with the inner side of the heel scraping along the floor. At the same time, both hands continue to circle respectively. The left hand swings leftward, upward,

then rightward, to the front of the right shoulder with the elbow bent; while the right hand moves leftward, downward, then rightward.

(105 - 107)

Turn your torso to the left and shift your weight leftward with the sole of the left foot placed fully on the floor. At the same time, the left hand drops, passing before the abdomen, then rises to

the front-left at chest level, with the elbow slightly bent, the wrist crooked, and the fingertips got together to form a hook; while the right hand swings upward and forward until it gets close to the right ear with the elbow bent, the palm facing the head and the fingers pointing to the rear-left.

(108 - 112)

Turn your torso to the right and shift your weight

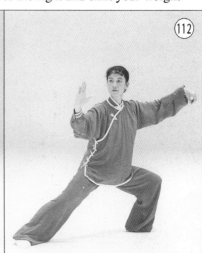

slightly rightward. Meanwhile, the right hand goes leftward and forward, then moves in a horizontal arc to the right side at shoulder level. Without any pause, turn your torso slightly to the left and shift your weight slightly leftward, and squat yourself down a little more. In coordination with the twist of the torso, lower both the shoulders with the arms well rounded and the elbows dropped. The right hand extends to the

front-right, forming a standing palm with the wrist sunk, the hollow of the hand obliquely facing forward and the fingers obliquely pointing upward. Simultaneously, the left hooked hand reaches to the front-left at shoulder level with the tip of the hook down. Look in the direction of the right hand.

Form 10
Lift and Retract

(113 - 115)

As you turn your torso slightly to the right and then back to the left, shift your weight slightly rightward. Along with the swift twist of the torso, both hands, with the left one changed back to a palm, swing upward, outward, downward and then press inward, drawing a small vertical circle respectively until they get to the front-left of the body with the left hand ahead, the right one about 10 cm beneath the inner side of the left elbow, and the thumb sides of the hands on top. Set your eyes on the left hand.

(116)

As you turn your torso slightly to the right and continue to shift your weight toward the right leg, draw the left foot back until the toes rest on the floor about 20 cm to the front-left of the right foot. At the same time, rotate both arms outward to turn the palms up, and withdraw both hands to the front of the abdomen, with the left hand a bit ahead, the right one beside the left elbow, and the fingers pointing to the front. Look to the lower-front.

(117 - 118)

Turn your torso slightly to the left and shift your weight completely onto the right leg. While straightening the right leg to stand up naturally, raise the left leg to waist level with the knee bent and the foot suspended. Meanwhile, with the

106

arms rotating inward, both hands rise a little and then push forward and downward until the left hand gets to the front of the left knee and the right one beside the inner side of the knee, with both palms facing the lower-front. Set your eyes on the left hand.

Form 11
Wade Forward

(119 - 120)

As you bend the right leg to squat yourself down and turn your torso to the right, the left foot lands and then shovels to the front-left with the toes tilted up and the inner side of the heel scraping along the floor. Meanwhile, both hands move downward, passing before the abdomen, then come to the right side of the body.

(121 - 122)

Turn your torso to the left and shift your weight toward the left leg with the sole of the foot placed fully on the floor. At the same time, the left hand continues to rise until the forearm lies crosswise in front of the chest with the palm obliquely facing backward; while the right hand swings up with the arm rotating outward, then pushes forward with the elbow bent, until the wrist clings to

the inner side of the left forearm. Eyes follow the right hand.

(123 - 125)

As you continue to turn round to the left, shift your weight completely onto the left leg. The right foot then takes a step, from beside the left one, to the front-right. Meanwhile, cross the arms in front of the chest with both forearms

107

rotated inward to turn the palms out. Then, raise both hands a little and separate them.

(126)

Turn your torso slightly to the right and shift your weight rightward to form a right-dominated horse-riding stance. At the same time, both hands go from the top to the sides at shoulder level respectively, with the shoulders lowered, the elbows dropped, the arms well rounded and the wrists sunk, thus forming standing palms with the hollows of the hands facing outward and the fingers pointing upward. Keep your waist relaxed and your hips lowered in the fixed position. Look in the direction of the right hand.

Form 12
Cover Hand and Thrust Fist — Right

(127 - 130)

Turn your torso slightly to the left and shift your weight slightly leftward. Meanwhile, both hands extend outward respectively, with the left arm rotating inward to turn the palm obliquely down and the right arm outward to turn the palm up.

(131 - 133)

As you turn your torso to the right and shift your weight completely onto the left leg, raise the right leg with the knee bent. The right foot then stamps on the floor with the left foot coming up swiftly. At the same time, the right hand changes

108

into a fist and, with the arm rotating inward and the elbow bent, swings upward and leftward, then drops to the front of the abdomen, the forefist obliquely facing downward; while the left hand sways upward with the arm rotating outward to turn the palm up, then rightward and downward with the elbow bent, until it lies upon the right forearm with the palm facing the right

and the forearm crosswise in front of the chest. Look to the lower-front.

(134 - 135)

As you bend the right leg to squat yourself down, the left foot shovels to the front-left with the inner side of the heel scraping along the floor. Meanwhile, both arms continue to apply joining forces in front of the chest and press a little down.

(136 - 137)

Turn your torso slightly to the right and shift your weight leftward with the left leg bent at the knee and the sole of the foot placed fully on the floor. Meanwhile, both arms separate and swing sideways up.

(138 - 140)

As you turn your torso slightly to the left and shift your weight slightly to the right, rotate both arms

outward. The left hand moves to the front of the left shoulder, with the elbow slightly bent, the thumb and the forefinger stretched out, the other three rolled up and the palm facing upward; while the right fist swings upward, inward and downward until it gets to the front of the chest with the elbow bent and the centre of the fist facing upward. Look in the direction of the left hand.

109

(141 - 143)

After you turn your torso slightly to the right and draw the right fist a little back to accumulate strength, turn your torso promptly to the left and shift your weight swiftly to the left to form a left bow stance, yet with the right leg slightly bent. At the same time, the left hand withdraws to the side of the torso with the hollow of the palm gently nestling against the left ribs; while the right fist, with the arm rotating inward to turn the centre of the fist down, thrusts quickly and explosively to the front-right at shoulder level. Look in the direction of the right fist.

Points for Attention: While punching, you should apply the strength from the waist, through the shoulder and the arm, and swiftly to the forefist.

Form 13
Punch with Body Draped Over

(144 - 147)

As you turn your torso slightly to the right and shift your weight slightly to the right, the left hand changes into a fist and, with the arm rotating inward, swings leftward, upward and forward until it gets to the front-left at forehead level with the arm rotated outward and the elbow slightly bent. Meanwhile, rotate the right arm outward and bend the elbow so as to draw the fist back beneath the inner side of the left elbow. Keep the centres of the fists obliquely upward.

110

(148 - 149)

As you continue to turn your torso to the right and shift your weight to the right, the left fist moves to the right, passing before the face, and then drops; while the right fist swings downward, passing before the abdomen, and then, with the arm rotating inward, comes up to the right side at shoulder level. Eyes follow the right fist.

(150 - 152)

Turn your torso to the left and shift your weight toward the left leg. At the same time, the left fist continues to move downward, passing before the abdomen, to the left side of the waist with the elbow bent and the centre of the fist facing upward; while the right fist, with the arm rotating outward, swings upward and inward until it gets

to the front of the right shoulder, the elbow bent and the centre of the fist facing backward. Look in the direction of the right fist.

Form 14
Lean with Back Twisted

(153 - 155)

As you twist your torso to the left and shift your

weight slightly leftward, rotate the left forearm inward to turn the centre of the fist down and place the forefist against the left side of the waist. Meanwhile, the right fist swings to the front of the left shoulder with the forearm rotating inward and the wrist protruding to the left. You ought to start the movement at high speed and gradually slow the pace.

111

(156 - 159)

Twist your torso to the right and shift your weight to the right, leaning with the back of your torso toward the rear-right. At the same time, with the right forearm continuing the inward rotation, the right fist sways in a counterclockwise circle and then parries to the upper-front-right of the forehead with the elbow bent and the centre of the fist facing outward. Keep the left forefist close against the side of the waist in the meantime. Set your eyes on the left foot.

Form 15
Blue Dragon Goes Out of Water

(160 - 162)

Turn your torso slightly to the left and shift your weight leftward. At the same time, the right fist swings forward with the forearm rotating outward; while the left fist stretches down and then rises from the left side with the arm rotating outward.

112

(163 - 165)

Turn your torso slightly to the right and shift your weight to the right. At the same time, the right fist swings downward, rightward and upward to shoulder level, the arm rotating first inward then outward; while the left fist continues to move upward, rightward and downward to the front of the chest. Eyes follow the left fist.

(166 - 167)

Turn your torso slightly to the left and shift your weight leftward. At the same time, the right fist continues to swing leftward until it gets to the front-right of the body with the elbow bent and the centre of the fist obliquely facing upward; while the left fist withdraws until it pauses before the left part of the abdomen. Eyes follow the right fist.

(168 - 170)

Turn your torso promptly to the right with the left foot driving backward to help exert strength. In coordination with the swift turn of the torso and the inward rotation of the left forearm, the left hand, with the thumb and the forefinger stretched out, the other three together rolled up slightly, springs explosively to the lower-front-right at abdomen level, the hollow of the hand obliquely facing downward, and force concentrated on the front part of the back of the hand. Simultaneously, the right fist swings leftward and downward, pausing just inside the left upper-arm. Look in the direction of the left hand.

(171 - 172)

Without any pause, turn your torso promptly to the left and shift your weight toward the right leg to form a right-dominated horse-riding stance with the hips lowered. Meanwhile, accompanied by the inward rotation of the forearm, the right fist springs explosively to the lower-front-right just above and in front of the right knee with the elbow slightly bent, the eye of the fist obliquely facing inward, and force concentrated on the little finger side of the fist. In coordination with the thrust of the right fist and at the same speed, the left hand withdraws until the palm nestles to the left part of the abdomen. Look in the direction of the right fist.

Points for Attention: While conducting the spring of the right fist and the withdrawal of the left palm during the last phase of this form, you

should exert your strength in opposite directions through the arms.

Form 16
Slice with Hand

(173 - 175)

Turn your torso slightly to the left and then back to the right. Meanwhile, shift your weight completely onto the left leg and raise the right leg with the knee bent. At the same time, the right fist changes back to a palm and swings backward, upward and forward round the elbow, the arm correspondingly rotating inward and then outward. Eyes follow the right palm.

(176)

As the right foot lands with the toes turned out, the right hand drops to the front of the abdomen

114

with the palm facing upward.

(177 - 179)

As you continue to turn round to the right, the left foot rises and then stamps on the floor next to the inner side of the right one. You thus take a full squat with both legs bent at the knees. At the same time, brandish your left arm. The left hand swings leftward, upward and forward, then slices down onto the right palm which is held crosswise in front of the body with the fingers pointing to the left. Concentrate force on the little finger side of the left palm and set your eyes on the left hand.

Form 17
Turn Flowers Out and Wave Sleeves

(180 - 181)

Rotate both arms inward and stretch both hands to the lower-left. As you turn your torso to the right, unbend both legs and then raise the right leg with the knee bent. Along with the turn of the body, both hands swing upward from the left side.

(182 - 184)

As you continue to turn to the right, the left foot drives the floor to jump up. The right foot and the left foot then land in succession, with the left one ahead, the knees bent and the weight predomi-

nantly kept on the right leg. At the same time, both hands continue to swing forward, and then slap down, ending with the left hand to the front-left of the torso at chest level, the right one in front of the abdomen, and both palms facing downward. Look in the direction of the left hand.

Form 18
Turn Flowers Out from Sea Bottom

(185 - 187)

Immediately after you turnd your torso slightly to the right, turn it back to the left promptly and explosively. Along with the twist of the body, shift your weight completely onto the unbent right leg and raise the left leg to abdomen level with the knee bent. At the same time, clench both your fists. The left fist swings downward, rightward, upward and leftward, then drops, drawing a vertical circle in front of the trunk, until it abruptly pauses about 10 cm outside the left knee, the arm slightly bent, the centre of the fist turned up, and the eye of the fist facing outward. Simultaneously, the right fist swings downward, rightward and upward until it gets to the upper-right of the head, the arm slightly bent and the centre of the fist facing to the left. Look in the direction of the left hand.

Form 19
Cover Hand and Thrust Fist — Left

(188 - 190)

As the left foot stamps on the floor, the right foot rises a little. At the same time, with the forearm rotating inward, the left fist swings upward, rightward, and then comes down to the front of the chest, the elbow bent and the forefist facing the lower-right; while the right hand changes back to a palm and drops from before the face, until it lies on the left forearm with the fingers pointing to the upper-left.

(191 - 193)

As you bend the left leg to squat yourself down, the right foot shovels to the front-right with the inner side of the heel scraping along the floor. Then, turn your torso slightly to the left and shift your weight rightward with the right leg bent at the knee and the sole of the foot placed fully on the floor. Meanwhile, both arms press down and separate. Both hands then swing sideways up respectively.

(194)

As you turn your torso slightly to the right and shift your weight slightly leftward, rotate both arms outward. The right hand moves to the front of the right shoulder with the elbow slightly bent, the thumb and the forefinger stretched out, the other three rolled up, and the hollow of the palm facing upward; while the left fist swings upward, inward and downward, until it comes to the front of the chest with the elbow bent and the centre of the fist facing upward.

(195 - 197)

After you turn your torso slightly to the left and draw the left fist a little back to accumulate strength, turn your torso promptly to the right and shift your weight swiftly rightward to form a right bow stance, yet with the left leg slightly

117

bent. At the same time, the right hand withdraws to the side of the torso with the hollow of the palm gently nestling against the right ribs; while the left fist, with the arm rotating inward to turn the centre of the fist down, thrusts quickly and explosively to the front-left at shoulder level. While punching, you should apply the strength from the waist, through the shoulder and the arm, and swiftly to the forefist. Look in the direction of the left fist.

Form 20
Six Sealings and Four Closings — Left

(198 - 200)
As you turn your torso slightly to the right and

shift your weight slightly to the right, the left fist changes back to a palm and pulls downward and rightward, then rises to the front-right of the chest with the elbow bent and the palm facing the rear-right. At the same time, rotate the right forearm inward and crook the hand down at the wrist. The right hand thus comes up with the palm facing the right and the thumb side of the hand gently scraping along the right ribs. The right hand then gets close to the left wrist.

(201)
Without any pause, as you turn your torso to the left and shift your weight leftward, both hands push to the front-left at shoulder level with the palms facing backward. Both hands then stretch further out, with the left forearm rotating inward and the right forearm slightly outward so as to

118

turn the left palm out and the right one obliquely up. Eyes follow the left hand.

(202 - 204)
Turn your torso to the right and shift your weight completely onto the right leg with the knee slightly bent and the toes turned out. Simultaneously, the left leg takes a step to the front-left with the knee slightly bent and the toes resting on the floor. Along with the turn of the body, the left hand moves downward, rightward and then upward, drawing a small vertical circle until it comes to the front-left again at a level slightly lower than the shoulder, the palm facing upward, the fingers pointing to the left and the elbow bent. Meanwhile, the right hand drops, passing before the chest, then rises to the upper-right beside the right ear with the elbow bent and the

wrist crooked. The little finger, ring finger and middle finger successively move in during the motion with the fingertips pointing obliquely to the ground. Look in the direction of the left palm.

(205 - 206)
Turn your torso to the right. Rotate both forearms inward to turn the palms up. Both hands simultaneously sway outward and backward until they respectively get close to the ears above the shoulders with the elbows bent.

(207 - 209)
As you turn your torso to the left, the left leg takes a step to the front-left. Then, shift your weight completely onto the left leg with the knee slightly bent, and bring the right foot forward with the toes resting on the floor about 20 cm to the side of the left heel, the knee slightly bent and turned out. Along with the turn of the body, both hands

119

press from above the shoulders to the lower-left beside the left hip, with the palms obliquely facing downward, the thumb and forefinger sides of the hands in opposition to each other. Look in the direction between the palms.

Form 21
Single Whip — Right

(210 - 226)
The same as described in Figures 57-70, but in the opposite direction, substituting "left" for "right" and vice versa. Besides, you should fin-

ish the form with an oblique Single Whip by moving the right foot obliquely to the right.

Stage Two
Form 22
Wave Hands like Clouds — Right

(227 - 231)

Immediately after you turn your torso slightly to the left and shift your weight leftward, turn the torso back to the right and shift the weight rightward. Simultaneously, the left hooked hand changes back to a palm. Along with the twist of the torso, both hands revolve round their own wrists downward, leftward, upward and rightward, thus drawing a small vertical circle respectively. Then, turn your torso to the left and shift your weight completely onto the left leg. Bring the right foot to about 20 cm beside the left one and rest the toes on the floor with the knee bent

121

and slightly turned out. At the same time, both hands continue to move rightward, downward and leftward until they get to the front-left of the body, with the left arm at shoulder level, the right hand at abdomen level, both palms facing outward and fingers pointing to the front-right. Look in the direction of the left hand.

(232)

As you continue to turn your torso slightly to the left and bend the left leg to squat yourself down a little more, the right leg takes a step to the right. Simultaneously, both hands push a little further to the front-left.

(233 - 235)

Turn your torso slightly to the right and shift your weight onto the slightly bent right leg. The left leg then takes a step from behind the right one to the rear-right with the ball of the foot resting on the floor. At the same time, rotate the right arm inward and the left arm outward. The right hand moves upward and rightward, passing before the chest, to the front-right with the palm facing outward and the fingers pointing to the upper-left; while the left hand swings downward and rightward, to the front-right of the abdomen with the palm facing outward and the fingers pointing to the front. Look in the direction of the right hand.

(236 - 237)

Turn your torso slightly to the left and shift your weight completely onto the slightly bent left leg. The right leg then takes a step to the right. At the same time, rotate the left arm inward and the right arm outward. The left hand moves upward and leftward, passing before the chest, to the front-left at a level slightly higher than the shoulder with the palm facing outward and the fingers pointing to the upper-right; while the right hand swings downward and leftward to the front-left of the abdomen with the palm facing outward and the fingers pointing to the front. Look in the direction of the left hand.

(238 - 240)

Turn your torso slowly to the right and shift your weight rightward with both legs further bent.

Accompanying the turn of the torso, with the arm rotating outward to turn the palm up, the left hand swings in a horizontal arc to the front-right, the elbow slightly bent. Meanwhile, the right hand moves upward with the arm rotating inward to turn the palm down, and then lies above the left upper-arm with the elbow bent. Eyes follow the left hand.

(241 - 242)

As you turn your torso slightly to the left and shift your weight slightly leftward, the left hand withdraws to the front of the chest; while the right hand reaches to the front-right from above the left palm.

(243 - 244)

Turn your torso promptly to the right and shift

123

your weight completely onto the unbent left leg. Raise the right leg to waist level with the knee bent. At the same time, with the arm rotated outward to turn the palm up, the right hand withdraws to the front of the abdomen; while the left hand, with the forearm rotated inward to turn the palm down, cuts explosively to the front-left from above the right palm, force concentrated on the little finger side of the palm. Look in the direction of the left hand.

Form 23
Wave Hands like Clouds — Left

(245 - 247)
As the right foot falls and stamps on the floor, the left heel rises with the knee bent. Then, as you turn your torso to the right, the right hand stretches to the front of the left shoulder with the arm rotating inward to turn the palm out; while the left hand drops with the arm rotating slightly outward, and begins to move to the right, the palm facing the right and the fingers pointing to the front. Look in the direction of the right hand.

(248 - 249)
As you continue to turn your torso to the right and bend the right leg to squat yourself down a little more, the left leg takes a step to the left. Along with the turn of the torso, the right hand moves in a horizontal arc, passing before the chest, to the front-right of the body at a level slightly higher than the shoulder with the palm facing outward and the fingers pointing to the upper-left; while the left hand continues to move, passing before the abdomen, to the front-right of the waist with the palm facing outward and the fingers pointing to the front-right. Look in the direction of the right hand.

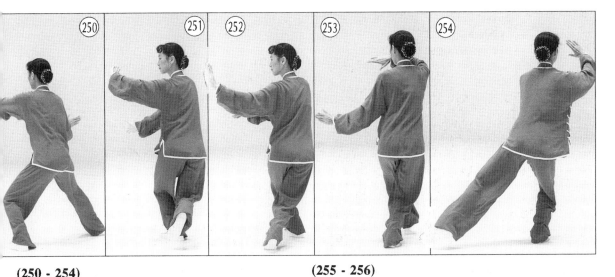

(250 - 254)

The same as described in Figures 233 - 237, only in the opposite direction, substituting "left" for "right" and vice versa.

Form 24
High Pat on Horse

(255 - 256)

Turn your torso to the left and shift your weight leftward with the toes of the left foot turned out. At the same time, with the left arm rotating inward, the left hand circles upward, leftward and then slightly downward. The right hand moves downward in the meantime. Both hands then swing inward with the arms rotating outward so that they get crossed in front of the chest

with the left one on top, the left palm facing the right, the right palm facing the left, the fingers all pointing to the front and the elbows slightly bent.

(257 - 260)

Shift your weight completely onto the left leg. The right foot goes forth, passing beside the left one, then shovels to the right with the inner side of the heel scraping along the floor. After that,

shift your weight to the right, with the sole of the right foot placed fully on the floor and the toes turned in. At the same time, rotate both arms inward to turn the palms out. Both hands respectively move to the sides at shoulder level, yet a little forward, with the elbows slightly bent, the wrists sunk, the palms facing outward and the fingers pointing obliquely upward. Eyes follow the right hand.

(261 - 263)
Turn your torso to the right and extend both hands with the arms rotating outward to turn the palms up. Correspondingly, the left arm sways a little forward.

(264 - 267)
As you turn your torso to the left, shift your weight completely onto the right leg with the toes of the foot turned in. Then, draw the left foot back with the toes resting on the floor about 20 cm beside the right heel, the knee slightly bent and turned out. Along with the turn of the body, the left hand withdraws to the front of the abdomen with the elbow bent, the palm facing upward and

the finger pointing to the right; while the right hand goes forth with the elbow bent, passing beside the right ear, then pushes to the front, thus forming a standing palm with the fingertips at nose level. Look in the direction of the right hand.

Form 25
Bombardments in Series — Right

(268 - 270)
As you turn your torso to the left, the right hand moves downward and leftward to the front of the left part of the abdomen; while the left hand rises a little.

126

(271)

As you turn your torso to the right, both hands continue to rise and then push to the front with the forearms overlapping and the right one out. Keep both hollows of the hands backward through the warding-off motion.

(272)

As you bend the right leg to squat yourself down,

the left leg takes a step to the rear-left. Meanwhile, both hands extend forward, with the right arm rotating inward to turn the palm obliquely out and the left arm slightly outward to turn the palm obliquely up.

(273 - 274)

As you turn your torso to the left and shift your weight onto the slightly bent left leg, raise the

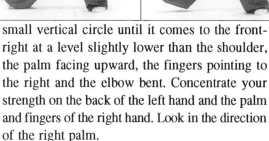

right heel with the toes of the foot still on the floor but twisted slightly leftward. At the same time, the left hand drops, and then rises to the upper-left beside the left ear with the elbow bent and the wrist crooked. The little finger, ring finger and middle finger successively move in during the motion with the fingertips pointing obliquely to the ground. Meanwhile, the right hand moves downward, leftward and then upward, drawing a

small vertical circle until it comes to the front-right at a level slightly lower than the shoulder, the palm facing upward, the fingers pointing to the right and the elbow bent. Concentrate your strength on the back of the left hand and the palm and fingers of the right hand. Look in the direction of the right palm.

(275 - 279)

As you turn your torso slightly to the left and

127

bend the left leg to squat yourself down, the right foot moves a bit to the right. Then, lower your hips with the waist relaxed and the buttocks held in. At the same time, rotate both forearms inward so that both hands respectively sway outward and upward until they move to the front of the chest with the elbows bent and the palms obliquely facing each other. Following the preceding movement, turn your torso to the right and shift your weight forward onto the right leg. The left foot coincidentally rises slightly off the floor and takes half a step forward with a drive. At the same time, rotate both arms inward to aggregate strength. Both hands thus push forcibly to the front. Hold the right arm at shoulder level with the palm obliquely facing forward and the fingers pointing to the upper-left, and the left hand at chest level with the palm facing forward and the

fingers pointing upward, and keep both elbows slightly bent in the fixed position. Look in the direction of the right hand.

(280 - 285)
Repeat the same movements as described in Figures 272 - 279.

128

Form 26
Bombardments in Series — Left

(286 - 287)

After the left leg takes half a step backward, shift your weight onto the left leg with the knee bent, and raise the right heel with the toes of the foot still on the floor. As you turn your torso to the left, rotate both arms outward. Both hands thus swing downward and leftward.

(288 - 289)

As you turn your torso to the right, the right leg takes a step backward. At the same time, both hands continue to swing upward. The moment the left hand rises to shoulder level and the right one to chest level, rotate the left forearm inward

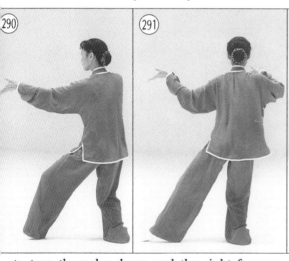

to turn the palm down and the right forearm outward to turn the palm up. Then, along with the turn of the body, both hands swing forward.

(290 - 291)

As you continue to turn round to the right, shift your weight onto the right leg with the knee bent, and raise the left heel with the left leg correspondingly rotating inward on the ball of the foot. At the same time, the right hand drops, and then rises to the upper-right beside the right ear with the elbow bent and the wrist crooked. The little finger, ring finger and middle finger successively move in during the motion with the fingertips pointing obliquely to the ground. Meanwhile, the left hand moves downward, rightward and then upward, drawing a small vertical circle until it comes to the front-left at a level slightly

129

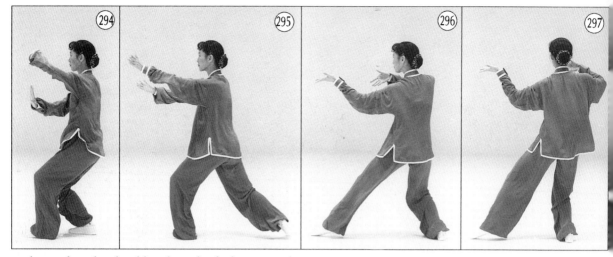

lower than the shoulder, the palm facing upward, the fingers pointing to the left and the elbow bent. Look in the direction of the left palm.

(292 - 300)
The same as described in Figures 275 - 285, only in the opposite direction, substituting "left" for "right" and vice versa.

Form 27
Flash the Back

(301 - 302)
As you turn your torso to the right and bend the right leg to squat yourself down a little more, bend the left leg at the knee and raise the left heel. At the same time, the right hand moves hori-zontally to the front-right of the chest with the elbow bent, the palm turned down and the fingers pointing to the front; while the left arm rotates slightly outward in front of the left shoulder, the elbow bent, the palm facing the front-right and the fingers pointing upward.

(303 - 306)

As you turn your torso to the left, the left leg takes half a step forward. Then, shift your weight forward to form a left bow stance yet with the right leg slightly bent. At the same time, the left hand swings rightward, downward and leftward until it gets beside the left hip with the palm turned down and the fingers pointing to the front; while the right hand continues to move rightward and downward, passing beside the waist, then with the forearm rotating outward to turn the palm up, stretches from above the left forearm to the upper-front at shoulder level with the elbow slightly bent, the palm obliquely facing upward and the fingers pointing to the upper-front.

(307 - 308)

Turn your torso slightly to the right and then back

to the left. Along with the small and swift twist of the torso, rotate the right arm inward so that the right hand revolves round the wrist rightward, backward and leftward, drawing a small horizontal circle with the palm finally turned out. The left hand stretches toward the rear-left in the meantime.

(309 - 310)

Turn your torso to the right and shift your weight to the right, with the toes of the left foot turned in. At the same time, with the arm rotating outward, the left hand swings upward from the left side. Along with the turn of the torso, the right hand moves round to the front of the trunk.

131

(311 - 315)

As you swiftly turn round about 180 degrees to the right using the ball of the left foot as a pivot, the right foot sweeps clockwise, completing a semicircle with the ball of the foot scraping along the floor. Then, set the foot firm on the floor about 30 cm behind the left heel and shift your weight backward. Keep both legs bent and the weight predominantly on the right leg. Along with the turn of the body, the right hand falls to the front of the right part of the abdomen with the elbow bent and the palm facing downward; while the left hand goes forth with the elbow bent, passing beside the left ear, then pushes to the lower-front-left with the elbow slightly bent, the wrist at chest level, the palm obliquely facing the right and the fingers pointing to the upper-front. **Points for Attention:** As the right heel stamps

on the floor with pausing power, you should exert great strength from your waist, bringing both hands to push promptly and explosively to the lower-front.

Stage Three
Form 28
Punch toward the Crotch

(316 - 318)

As you turn your torso to the right, the left hand swings slightly upward with the forearm rotating outward, then rightward and downward with the

forearm rotating inward to turn the palm down; while the right hand moves downward and rightward with the forearm rotating outward to turn the palm up, then rises to the shoulder level.

(319 - 321)

As you turn your torso slightly to the left and shift your weight completely onto the left leg with the knee slightly bent, raise the right leg to abdomen level with the knee bent and the foot naturally suspended. At the same time, the left hand continues to circle downward and leftward, then rises with the forearm rotating outward, and moves rightward until it gets to the front-left of the head with the elbow bent, the palm facing rightward and the fingers obliquely pointing upward; while the right hand changes into a fist and continues to move upward and leftward to

the front of the neck with the elbow bent and the wrist crooked to turn the forefist obliquely down.

(322)

As the right foot falls and stamps on the floor, raise the left heel with the knee of the leg bent. At the same time, both hands continue to move inward and downward until the forearms overlap in front of the chest with the left one on top.

(323)

As you bend the right leg to squat yourself down, the left foot rises a little and then shovels to the front-left with the inner side of the heel scraping along the floor. Meanwhile, both arms continue to exert joining forces, with the left palm facing the lower-right and the fingers pointing to the upper-right, and the centre of the right fist facing downward. Set your eyes on the left hand.

(324 - 326)

Shift your weight leftward with the left leg bent at the knee and the sole of the foot placed fully on the floor. Meanwhile, both arms separated and swing sideways up.

(327 - 328)

As you turn your torso slightly to the left and shift your weight slightly rightward, rotate both arms outward. The left hand continues to swing rightward until it gets to the front of the left shoulder with the elbow bent, the thumb and the forefinger naturally stretched out, the other three rolled up, and the hollow of the palm facing upward; while the right fist swings upward and leftward until it comes to the front of the right shoulder with the elbow bent and the centre of the fist facing backward.

(329 331)

After you turn your torso slightly to the right and draw the right fist a little back to accumulate strength, turn your torso promptly to the left and shift your weight swiftly leftward to form a left bow stance, yet with the right leg slightly bent. At the same time, the left hand moves rightward and downward, then withdraws to the left side with the hollow of the palm gently nestling against the abdomen; while the right fist swings slightly leftward and downward with the arm rotating inward, then springs explosively from above the

left palm to the lower-front-left at crotch level, the elbow slightly bent and the centre of the fist obliquely facing downward. Look in the direction of the right fist.

Points for Attention: The twines of the arms should be harmonious and smooth, as well as in tune with the nimble twist of the torso. Moreover, the spring of the right fist and the withdrawal of the left palm should be well coordinated with the prompt turn of the torso.

Form 29
White Ape Presents Fruit

(332 - 337)

After you turn your torso slightly to the left, turn it back to the right and shift your weight rightward. Along with the twist of the torso, the right fist circles, first leftward with the forearm rotating inward, then upward from the left side, and then rightward passing before the forehead, and finally downward to the right side of the waist with the forearm rotating outward to turn the centre of the fist up. Meanwhile, the left hand revolves round the wrist, first downward and backward with the wrist crooked, then upward with the thumb and the forefinger gently clinging to the torso, and finally forward with the forearm rotating outward, thus drawing a small complete

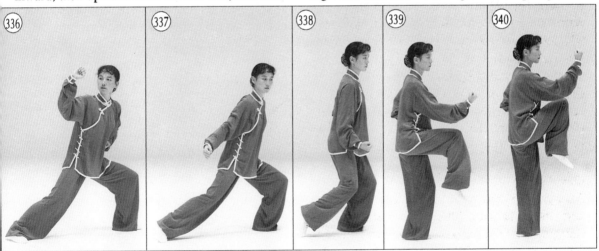

circle clockwise against the surface of the abdomen. In coordination with the revolution of the left hand, the left elbow sways forward and then backward.

(338 - 340)

As you turn your torso to the left and shift your weight completely onto the left leg with the knee unbent, raise the right leg to abdomen level with the knee bent and the foot naturally suspended. At the same time, the right fist continues to swing forward and upward until it pauses in front of and slightly higher than the right shoulder with the elbow bent and the centre of the fist facing the upper-rear; while the left hand changes into a fist and withdraws to the left side of the waist with the centre of the fist facing upward. Look in the direction of the right fist.

Form 30
Push with Both Hands

(341 - 344)

As you turn your torso to the left and bend the left leg to take a half squat, the right foot lands to the front-right with the weight predominantly on the left leg. Meanwhile, with both fists opened, the left hand rises to the front-left of the chest. Without any pause, rotate both forearms inward. Both hands thus sway outward and backward until they respectively get close to the ears above the shoulders with the elbows bent and the palms obliquely facing upward.

(345 347)

Turn your torso to the right and shift your weight

completely onto the right leg with the knee slightly bent. Bring the left foot about 20 cm beside the right one with the toes resting on the floor, the knee bent and turned out, thus forming a left empty stance. Along with the turn of the body, both hands press a little down to form standing palms, and then push to the front with the wrists at chest level, the palms obliquely facing each other and the fingers all pointing upward. Look in the direction between the hands.

Form 31
Mid-level Skill

(348 - 350)

Turn your torso slightly to the right. At the same time, rotate the right arm outward and strengthen

136

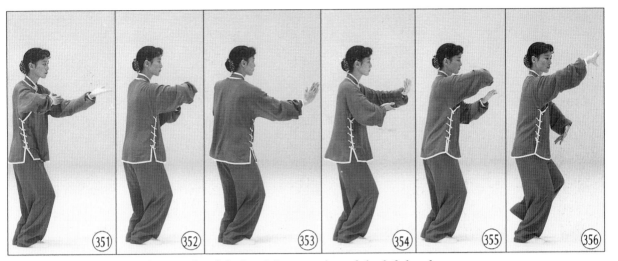

(351) (352) (353) (354) (355) (356)

the wrist to turn the palm up. The right hand then withdraws to the front of the chest with the elbow bent and the fingers pointing to the left. Simultaneously, rotate the left arm inward so as to hold a thwartwise palm. The left hand then pushes from above the right palm to the front with the elbow slightly bent, the palm facing the lower-front and the fingers pointing to the right. Look in the direction of the left hand.

(351 - 352)
Turn your torso slightly to the left. At the same time, with the left forearm rotated outward to turn the palm up, the left hand moves slightly downward and backward. Correspondingly, with the right forearm rotated inward to turn the palm down, the right hand moves slightly upward and forward from above the left palm. Both hands therefore roll in front of the chest with the palms facing each other. Look in the direction of the right hand.

(353 - 354)
Turn your torso slightly to the right. At the same time, with the right forearm rotated outward to turn the palm up, the right hand moves slightly downward and backward. Correspondingly, with the left forearm rotated inward to turn the palm down, the left hand moves slightly upward and forward from above the right palm. Both hands therefore roll once more in front of the chest with the palms facing each other. Look in the direc-

tion of the left hand.

Points for Attention: Along with the turn of the torso and the roll of the hands, the left foot should twist correspondingly leftward and rightward on its toes.

(355)
As you turn your torso slightly to the left, rotate the left forearm outward and the right forearm inward so as to turn the left palm up and the right palm down. Simultaneously, the right hand stretches leftward, upward and forward, From above the left forearm to the shoulder level, the fingers pointing to the front-left; while the left hand moves rightward and downward until it comes about 20 cm beneath the right elbow with the fingers pointing to the right.

(356 - 358)
Turn your torso slightly to the right and raise the left leg with the knee bent. Then, as the left foot stamps on the floor, the right foot rises a little. At the same time, both hands continue to circle respectively. The right hand swings forward, rightward and downward to the front-right at abdomen level; while the left hand moves downward, leftward and upward to the front-left at shoulder level.

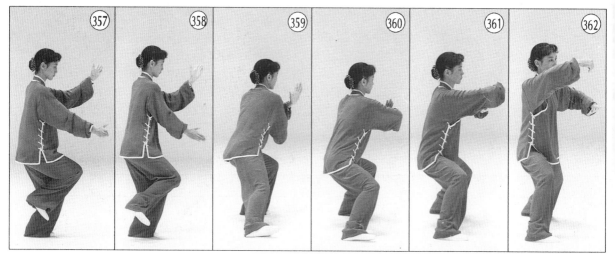

(359)

As you bend the left leg to squat yourself down a little more, the right foot shovels to the right with the inner side of the heel scraping along the floor. At the same time, both hands press inward until the right hand moves to the front of the left hip with the palm facing the upper-rear, the fingers pointing to the lower-front-left, and the left hand comes to the front of the right shoulder

above the right upper-arm with the palm facing rightward, the fingers pointing to the upper-right. Look in the direction of the right hand.

(360 - 365)

Shift your weight rightward and keep it predominantly on the right leg with the sole of the foot placed fully on the floor and the toes turned in. At the same time, the left hand moves slightly

forward, then downward and leftward until it pauses about 20 cm above the left knee with the palm obliquely facing downward; while the right hand moves slightly forward, then upward and rightward until it comes to the front-right at a level slightly higher than the head, with the thumb naturally stretched out, and the other four successively rolled into the hollow of the palm which faces the lower-left. Lower your hips in

the fixed position and look horizontally forward.

Form 32
The Former Trick

(366)

Immediately after you turn your torso slightly to the right, turn it a little back to the left and shift your weight slightly leftward. Meanwhile, rotate

the right forearm inward and expand the fingers. In coordination with the twist of the torso, both hands revolve round their own wrists rightward, then upward and leftward, drawing a small circle respectively.

(367 - 369)
As you turn your torso to the right and shift your weight onto the right leg with the knee bent, the left foot takes half a step to the front-left with the toes resting on the floor to form a left empty stance. At the same time, the right hand continues to swing leftward, downward, then rightward and upward, moving along a small arc until it comes to the front-right of the forehead with the palm facing outward and the fingers pointing to the left; while the left hand moves leftward, then following the advance of the left leg swings

forward and rightward until it pauses about 10 cm in upper-front of the left knee with the palm facing the lower-rear and the fingers pointing to the lower-front. Look in the direction of the left hand.

Form 33
The Latter Trick

(370 - 374)
The left foot moves a little further to the front-left. As you then turn your torso to the left and shift your weight onto the left leg with the knee bent and the sole of the foot placed fully on the floor, the right foot takes a step to the front-right with the knee bent and the toes resting on the floor to form a right empty stance. At the same time, the left hand swings rightward and upward,

passing before the chest, then moves to the front-left of the forehead, the forearm rotating inward to turn the palm out with the fingers pointing to the right; while the right hand moves rightward and downward, then following the advance of the right leg, swings forward and leftward until it pauses about 10 cm in upper-front of the right knee with the palm facing the lower-rear and the fingers pointing to the lower-front. Look in the direction of the right hand.

Form 34
Part the Wild Horse's Mane — Right

(375 - 376)
Turn your torso to the right. At the same time, the left hand moves leftward and downward, then swings forward from beside the left thigh with the forearm rotating outward, the palm facing the front and the fingers pointing to the ground; while the right hand moves leftward and upward, passing before the chest, then swings rightward with the forearm rotating inward until it comes to the front-right of the forehead with the palm facing outward and the fingers pointing to the left.

(377 - 380)
As you turn your torso to the left, raise the right leg to abdomen level with the knee bent and the

foot naturally suspended. At the same time, the left hand continues to swing rightward, upward and leftward, passing before the chest with the forearm rotating inward, until it comes to the left side with the wrist slightly higher than the shoulder level, the palm facing outward and the fingers pointing to the upper-front-left; while the right hand moves rightward, downward, forward and upward with the forearm rotating outward, reaching to the front above the right knee with the palm facing upward and the fingers pointing to the front-right. Look in the direction of the right hand.

(381 - 382)
As you bend the left leg to squat down, the right foot falls and then shovels to the front-right with the inner side of the heel scraping along the floor. Then, shift your weight toward the right leg with the knee bent and the sole of the foot placed fully on the floor, thus forming a right-dominated horse-riding stance. At the same time, the left arm expands a little outward; while the right hand stretches further to the upper-front until the fingers get to nose level with the palm facing the rear-right. Look in the direction of the right hand.

Form 35
Part the Wild Horse's Mane — Left

(383 - 384)
As you turn your torso slightly to the left, both hands swing round their own wrists rightward, upward and then leftward, drawing a small arc respectively.

(385 - 387)
As you turn your torso to the right and shift your weight onto the right leg with the toes of the foot turned out, raise the left leg to abdomen level with the knee bent and the foot naturally suspended. At the same time, the left hand moves downward, forward and upward with the fore-

arm rotating outward, reaching to the front above the left knee with the palm facing upward; while the right hand swings rightward with the forearm rotating inward, until it comes to the right side with the wrist slightly higher than the shoulder level, the palm facing outward and the fingers pointing to the upper-front-right. Look in the direction of the left hand.

(388 - 391)
As you bend the right leg to squat down, the left foot falls and then shovels to front-left with the inner side of the heel scraping along the floor. Then, shift your weight toward the left leg with the knee bent and the sole of the foot placed fully on the floor, thus forming a left-dominated horse-riding stance. At the same time, the right arm expands a little outward; while the left hand

stretches further to the upper-front until the fingers get to nose level with the palm facing the rear-left. Look in the direction of the left hand.

Form 36
Swing Lotus and Drop into Splits

(392 - 394)

Turn your torso slightly to the left and shift your weight slightly leftward. At the same time, the left hand stretches further to the front-left with the wrist at shoulder level; while the right arm moves horizontally forward and leftward. Then, turn your torso slightly to the right and shift your weight slightly rightward. Meanwhile, bend both elbows with the left forearm rotating inward and the right one outward so that both hands sway round their own wrists leftward, backward and

then rightward, moving along a small arc respectively, until they come above the shoulders with the palms facing upward and the fingers pointing to the rear.

(395)

As you continue to turn your torso to the right and shift your weight toward the right leg, the right hand reaches to the front-right with the elbow unbent, the wrist slightly higher than the shoulder level and the palm facing outward; while the left hand moves rightward and downward to the front of the right part of the chest with the palm obliquely facing downward.

(396)

Without any pause, turn your torso promptly to the left and shift your weight swiftly toward the

142

left leg. Correspondingly, both hands pull explosively downward and leftward, ending with the left hand in front of the left side of the waist and the right one in front of the right hip, both palms obliquely facing downward and the fingers pointing the lower-right. Look in the direction of the right hand.

(397 - 398)

As you continue to turn your torso to the left and shift your weight leftward, both hands go on swing leftward, forward and upward to chest level with palms facing downward.

(399 - 401)

As you turn your torso to the right and shift your weight onto the left leg, bring the right foot next to the left one with the toes resting on the floor.

Meanwhile, both hands move horizontally to the right and then drop a little, ending with the right hand to the side of the body at waist level and the left one in front of the right part of the chest. Keep both hands a little more than a shoulder-width apart from each other during the motion. Look in the direction of the right hand.

(402 - 405)

Keep your weight completely on the left leg with the knee slightly bent. The right foot swings toward the upper-left and then sweeps round from the left to the right in a fan-shaped arc with the knee naturally straightened. Meanwhile, both hands swing upward and leftward, slapping the instep of the right foot successively in front of the chest (the left hand first, and then the right).

143

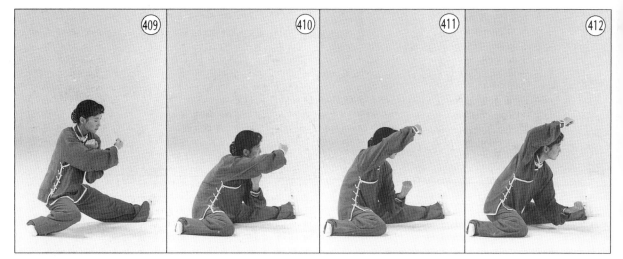

Eyes follow the right hand.

(406 - 407)

Bend the left leg to squat yourself down a little more. As the right foot falls and stamps on the floor next to the left one, the left foot immediately rises. At the same time, clench both your fists. The right fist moves to the front with the eye of the fist on top; while the left fist withdraws to the front of the right part of the chest with the elbow bent.

(408 - 413)

As you bend the right leg to squat down, the left foot shovels to the front-left with the toes tilted up and the heel scraping along the floor. Then, with the hips relaxed and the right knee pressing inward, the body drops until the buttocks, the

inner side of the right leg and the back of the leg are placed on the floor. At the same time, the right fist swings upward and rightward, passing before the face, to the upper-right above the right shoulder with the arm well rounded and the centre of the fist turned out; while the left fist goes on moving downward, and then stretches along the inner side of the left leg to the front-left with the centre of the fist facing upward. Look in the direction of the left fist.

Form 37
Golden Cock Stands on Single Leg — Left and Right

(414 - 416)

As the body goes up with the right foot driving

144

the floor, bend the left leg at the knee and shift your weight forward to form a left bow stance. Simultaneously, the left fist moves a little forward and upward with the forearm rotating inward until it gets to a level slightly lower than the shoulder. The right fist falls in the meantime.

(417 - 422)

Turn your torso to the left and shift your weight completely onto the left leg. As you slightly unbend the left leg to stand up, raise the right leg to abdomen level with the knee bent and the foot naturally suspended. At the same time, open both fists. The left hand moves rightward until it comes thwartwise in front of the chest with the elbow bent, the palm turned down and the fingers pointing to the right, then continues to press down to the side of the left hip with the palm

obliquely facing downward. Simultaneously, the right hand goes on swinging downward and forward, passing beside the right hip, then penetrates upward from inside the left forearm with the palm facing the rear-right. While the hand is moving before the face, rotate the forearm inward. The right hand thus continues to stretch to the upper-right with the palm facing the right. Look horizontally forward.

(423)

As you bend the left leg to squat yourself down a little, the right foot falls and stamps on the floor about 20 cm beside the left one. Meanwhile, the left hand rises a little. Both hands then press down to the front of the abdomen with the palms facing downward and the fingers pointing to the front.

145

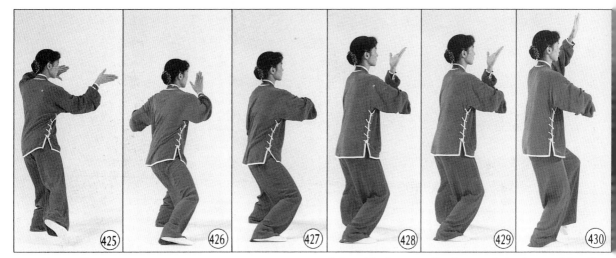

(424)

Turn your torso slightly to the right and shift your weight slightly rightward. Meanwhile, both hands swing downward and rightward.

(425)

As you turn your torso to the left and shift your weight onto the left leg with the knee further bent, the right foot rises and then shovels to the right with the toes tilted up and the inner side of the heel scraping along the floor. At the same time, with the left arm rotating inward and the right one outward, both hands swing upward, forward and leftward, until the left hand comes to the front-left at shoulder level and the right hand to the front at chest level with the palms facing the front-left and the fingers pointing to the front-right.

(426 - 432)

Turn your torso slightly to the right and shift your weight completely onto the right leg. Bring the left foot next to the right one with the toes resting on the floor. Then, as you slightly unbend the right leg to stand up, raise the left leg to abdomen level with the knee bent and the foot naturally suspended. At the same time, the right hand moves leftward until it comes thwartwise in front of the chest with the elbow bent, the palm turned down and the fingers pointing to the left, then continues to press down to the side of the right hip with the palm obliquely facing downward. Simultaneously, the left hand on swing downward to the side of the left hip with the palm turned up and the fingers pointing to the front, then penetrates upward from inside the right forearm with the palm facing the rear-left. While

146

the hand is moving before the face, rotate the forearm inward. The left hand thus continues to stretch to the upper-left with the palm facing the left. Look horizontally forward.

(437 - 438)
Shift your weight slightly leftward and rotate both arms outward to turn the palms up.

Stage Four
Form 38
Step Back and Roll Arms

(433 - 435)
As you bend the right leg to squat yourself down, the left foot drops, passing beside the inner side of the right calf, then steps to the rear-left. At the same time, the left hand falls, passing before the face to the front of the chest; while the right hand moves upward and then stretches from the left forearm to the front.

(436)
As you turn torso to the left, shift your weight slightly leftward to form a right-dominated horse-riding stance. At the same time, the left hand continues to move a little downward, leftward, then upward to the front-left at a level slightly lower than the shoulder with the palm facing outward and the fingers pointing to the front-left; while the right hand extends to the front-right at a level slightly lower than the shoulder with the palm facing outward and the fingers pointing to the front-right. Look in the direction of the left hand.

(439 - 441)

Shift your weight onto the left leg with the knee bent. As you turn round to the right, the right foot retreats to the rear-right, passing beside the left one and moving in an arc, with the sole gently scraping along the floor. Along with the turn of the body, the right hand moves leftward with the forearm rotating inward until it comes thwartwise in front of the chest with the palm obliquely facing downward; while the left hand rolls up with the elbow bent, and then pushes forward, passing beside the left ear and then from above the right forearm, the palm facing the front.

(442 - 443)

As you go on turning your torso to the right, shift your weight slightly rightward with both legs bent to form a left-dominated horse-riding stance.

At the same time, the right hand continues to move a little downward, rightward, then upward to the front-right at a level slightly lower than the shoulder with the palm facing outward and the fingers pointing to the front-right; while the left hand extends to the front-left at a level slightly lower than the shoulder with the palm facing outward and the fingers pointing to the front-left. Look in the direction of the right hand.

(444 - 445)

Shift your weight slightly rightward and rotate both arms outward to turn the palms up.

148

(446 - 449)

Shift your weight onto the right leg with the knee bent. As you turn round to the left, the left foot retreats to the rear-left, passing beside the right one and moving in an arc, with the sole gently scraping along the floor. Along with the turn of the body, the left hand moves rightward with the forearm rotating inward until it comes thwartwise in front of the chest with the palm obliquely facing downward; while the right hand rolls up with the elbow bent, and then pushes forward, passing beside the right ear then from above the left forearm, the palm facing the front.

(450)

Shift your weight slightly leftward with both legs bent to form a right-dominated horse-riding stance. At the same time, the left hand continues

to move downward to the front of the abdomen with the palm facing downward and fingers pointing to the right; while the right hand extends to the front-right at a level slightly higher than the shoulder with the palm facing outward and the fingers pointing to the front-left.

Form 39
Step Back and Press Elbow

(451)

As you turn your torso further to the left and shift your weight toward the left leg, the left hand goes leftward and upward; while the right hand moves slightly downward, and then leftward with the arm rotating outward to turn the palm up.

(452 - 453)

As the left hand extends to the front-left of the

149

body at chest level with the arm rotating outward, bend the right elbow and rotate the right forearm inward so that the right swings to the front of the right shoulder with the palm obliquely facing downward. Without any pause, turn your torso to the right and shift your weight toward the right leg. Brought along by the turning torso, the left hand moves horizontally forward and rightward with the palm facing the right. The right hand swings to the front-right with the forearm rotating further inward to turn the palm out in the meantime. Look in the direction of the left hand.

(454 - 456)
As you turn your torso slightly to the left and shift your weight onto the left leg, draw the right foot backward with the heel raised and the ball scrap-

ing along the floor. At the same time, bend the left elbow and rotate the left forearm inward. The left hand thus swings rightward until it comes thwartwise in front of the chest with the tip of the elbow pointing to the front-left, and then rises with the fingers hanging down naturally. Simultaneously, the right hand swings horizontally leftward with the arm rotating outward until it comes about 10 cm beneath the left elbow with

the palm facing upward and the fingers pointing to the front-left.

(457 458)
As you turn your torso to the right, the right foot continues to retreat to the rear-right, passing beside the left one and moving in an arc, with the heel raised and the ball scraping along the floor, and then stamps on the floor. After that, shift

150

your weight backward and keep it predominantly on the right leg with the knee slightly bent. At the same time, the right hand withdraws swiftly to the front of the right part of the abdomen with the palm facing upward and the fingers pointing to the front-left; while the left hand cuts explosively from above the right arm to the front-left at chest level, with the palm facing downward, the fingers pointing to the front-right, and the force concentrated on the little finger side of the palm. Look in the direction of the left hand.

Form 40
Rub Instep

(459)
Turn your torso to the right and shift your weight rightward. Both hands swing downward and rightward in the meantime.

(460 - 464)
As you turn your torso slightly to the left and shift your weight onto the left leg, the right foot takes a step across the left one to the front-left with the toes turned out, thus forming a half squat with the legs bent and crossed and the left heel raised. At the same time, the left hand continues to swing rightward with the forearm rotating outward, passing before the abdomen, then rises with the forearm rotating inward, ending with the forearm thwartwise in front of the chest with the elbow bent, the palm facing downward, and the fingers pointing to the right; while the right hand circles rightward and upward, then leftward and downward with the forearm rotating inward, until the forearm lies upon the left forearm with the elbow bent, the palm facing downward and the fingers pointing to the left. Look to the left.

(465 - 467)

As you shift your weight completely onto the right leg with the knee extended to stand up, the left leg swings up so that the foot kicks to the upper-front-left with the ankle straightened and the knee unbent swiftly. At the same time, both hands swing upward, then separate from top to the sides respectively, ending with the left hand slapping the instep of   the left foot to the

upper-front-left, and the right hand coming to the upper-right of the torso with the palm facing outward and the fingers pointing upward. Look in the direction of the left hand.

Form 41
Kick Sideward with Right Foot

(468 - 471)

As you turn your torso to the right, the left leg falls with the knee bent. The left foot then lands outside the right one with the toes turned in. You thus continue to turn round about 180 degrees to the right on balls of the feet. Along with the turn of the body, both hands swing downward and inward with the palms gradually changing into fists, until they cross in front of the abdomen with

the left fist out, the eyes of the fists facing forward.

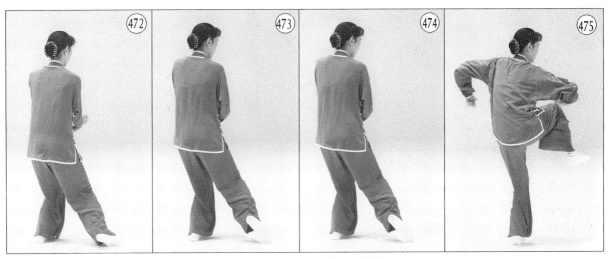

(472 - 473)

Shift your weight onto the left leg with the knee slightly bent and raise the right heel with the toes of the foot still resting on the floor. Meanwhile, both fists swing forward, outward, downward and inward, drawing a small completely circle respectively, ending with the wrists crossed in front of the abdomen again, with the eyes of the fists facing forward and the right fist out.

(474 - 476)

Without any pause, raise the right leg with the knee bent. The right foot kicks explosively to the upper-right at waist level with the toes turned in, the knee unbent swiftly, and the force concentrated on the outer side of the foot. At the same time, both fists explosively swing outward and upward to the right and the left sides at shoulder level respectively, with centres of the fists ob-

liquely facing downward. Look in the direction of the right fist.

Form 42
Turn Flowers Out from Sea Bottom

(477 - 479)

As you bend the left leg to squat yourself down

a little, the right leg falls with the knee bent. At the same time, the left fist swings upward and rightward, then drops to the front of the chest with the elbow bent and the centre of the fist facing downward; while the right fist moves downward and leftward with the forearm rotating inward, passing beside the inner side of the right knee to the front of the abdomen.

(480 - 481)

As you turn your torso promptly to the right and extend the left leg to stand up, raise the right leg to waist level with the knee bent and the foot naturally suspended. At the same time, the left fist goes on dripping from before the abdomen, then swings leftward and upward explosively, with the forearm rotating outward, until it gets to the upper-front-left at a level slightly higher than the head with the elbow bent and the centre of the fist facing the right. Simultaneously, the right fist continues to rise from inside the left forearm, then swings rightward from before the face, and finally drops with the forearm rotating outward, until it abruptly pauses about 10 cm outside the right knee with the elbow bent and the centre of the fist facing upward. Look in the direction of the right fist.

Form 43
Punch toward the Ground

(482 - 483)

As you turn your torso slightly to the right and bend the left leg to squat yourself down a little, the right foot lands to the front with the knee bent. Then, shift your weight forward. Along with the turn of the torso, the left fist swings forward and downward with the arm rotating outward; while the right fist swings downward, backward and then upward. Look in the direction of the left hand.

(484 - 486)

As you go on shifting your weight forward with the right foot driving the floor to leap, the left foot

154

takes a step to the front. The right foot immediately swings forward before the left foot lands, until it comes beside the left calf with the knee bent. Simultaneously, turn your torso to the left. The left fist continues to swing downward and backward, passing beside the left hip, then rises from the rear-left and moves to the front-left with the elbow bent; while the right fist continues to move upward, forward, leftward and downward,

circling counterclockwise.

(487 - 490)
After the right foot shovels to the front-right with the inner side of the heel scraping along the floor, turn your torso to the right and shift your weight toward the right leg with the knee bent and the sole of the foot placed fully on the floor to form a right bow stance. Along with the turn of the

torso, the right fist continues to circle rightward and upward until it gets to the right side of the head with the elbow bent and the centre of the fist facing downward; while the left fist plunges to the lower-front-left at abdomen level with the forearm rotating inward. Look in the direction of the left fist.

Form 44
Turnover and Jump Slap Kick

(491 - 497)
Shift your weight leftward with the toes of the right foot turned in. As you then round about 180 degrees to the left, shift your weight back onto the right leg with the knee slightly bent. The left

155

foot coincidentally moves a little leftward with the toes resting on the floor. Along with the turn of the body, the left fist circles upward, leftward and downward until it gets to the front of the left hip with the centre of the fist facing upward; while the right fist drops to the side of the right hip and then rises sideways to the upper-right at a level slightly higher than the head with the centre of the fist facing the left. Look horizon-tally forward.

(498 - 500)

Shift your weight onto the left leg with the heel set firm on the floor. As you turn your torso slightly to the left, the right fist goes forward and downward with the forearm rotating outward; while the left fist swings downward and back-ward, passing beside the left hip, then rises from

the rear-left.

(501 - 502)

The right foot takes a step forward. Shift your weight toward the right leg with the knee bent. At the same time, the right fist continues to circle downward and backward, then rises from the rear-right; while the left fist goes on swinging upward, forward and downward to the front of

the left shoulder.

(503 - 505)

As the left leg swings forward and upward with the knee bent, the right foot drives the floor to jump into air. The right leg then swings forward and upward so that the foot explosively kicks to the upper-front with the ankle straightened and the knee unbent swiftly. At the same time, open

both your fists. The right hand continues to swing upward, forward and downward, slapping the instep of the right foot at chest level; while the left hand moves downward, and then rises from the left side to the shoulder level with the palm facing downward. Look in the direction of the right hand.

Form 45
Double Stamps with Feet

(506 - 510)

As the left foot lands on the floor, the right leg falls with the knee bent. The left foot immediately drives the floor to leap backward. The right foot then lands on the floor and the left foot

follows to the rear. At the same time, both hands respectively move to the right and the left sides at shoulder level with the palms facing outward. Look horizontally forward.

(511 - 513)

As you turn your torso slightly to the left and shift your weight backward onto the left leg with the knee slightly bent, the right foot retreats a little

with the toes resting on the floor to form a right empty stance. Meanwhile, both hands respectively move downward and inward with the arms rotating outward, then rise to the front of the chest with the right hand ahead, the left one beside the right elbow, and the palms facing upward.

157

(514 - 515)
Bend both knees further so as to squat yourself down a little more with the sole of the right foot placed fully on the floor. Meanwhile, both hands press slightly downward and forward to abdomen level with the arms rotating inward to turn the palms down.

(516 - 517)
While the right leg swings up with the knee bent, the left foot drives the floor to jump into the air. Meanwhile, rotate both arms outward to turn the palms up and hold both hands up with the right wrist slightly higher than the shoulder level and the left hand beside the right elbow. Both arms exert aggregating strength throughout the motion.

(518 - 519)
While landing, the left foot stamps on the floor with a smack, and so does the right foot in succession. Simultaneously, both hands press down to chest level with the arms rotating inward to turn the palms down, the right hand ahead and the left one beside the right elbow. Look in the direction of the right hand.

158

Form 46
Kick with Right Heel

(520 - 524)

As you shift your weight completely onto the left leg with the knee straightened to stand up, raise the right leg with the knee bent. Meanwhile, both hands withdraw to the front of the abdomen with the arms slightly rotating outward. The right foot then explosively kicks to the front-right at a level higher than the waist, with the toes tilted up, the knee unbent swiftly, and the force concentrated on the heel. At the same time, the right hand pushes to the front-right at shoulder level with the elbow slightly bent, forming a standing palm with the fingers pointing upward. Simultaneously, the left hand moves upward with the arm rotating

inward until it gets to the upper-left of the head with the elbow bent, the palm obliquely facing upward. Look in the direction of the right hand. Immediately after the kick, bend the right leg at the knee with the aid of the rebounding force.

Form 47
Jade Girl Works at Shuttles

(525 - 526)

As the right foot lands to the front-right with the toes slightly turned out, the right hand reaches horizontally forward with the palm turned down. Simultaneously, the left hand drops to the upper-front of the left shoulder with the elbow bent and the palm facing outward.

(527 - 528)

With the left leg swinging forward, the right foot drives the floor to leap forward. As you turn to the right in the air, the left leg hand pushes swiftly to the left side at shoulder level with the fingers pointing upward; while the right hand moves rightward and upward until it gets to the upper-right of the head with the palm obliquely facing upward. Look in the direction of the left hand.

(529)

After the left foot lands, the right foot takes a step from behind the left leg to the rear-left with the ball resting on the floor. Bend both knees and keep the weight predominantly on the left.

Form 48
Smooth Elbow Butt

(530 - 531)

As you turn round about 180 degrees to the right with the toes of the left foot turned in, shift your weight toward the right leg.

(532 - 534)

As you shift your weight onto the left leg with the knee slightly bent, raise the right heel with the toes still resting on the floor. The right hand moves rightward and downward with the elbow slowly unbent in the meantime.

160

(535 - 537)

As you turn your torso slightly to the left and bend the left leg at the knee to squat yourself down a little more, the right foot shovels to the right with the inner side of the heel scraping along the floor. At the same time, the right arm continues to swing downward and leftward, ending with the hand above the left knee, the elbow extended, and the palm facing the left; while the

left hand moves rightward until it gets to the front of the right shoulder with the elbow bent, the palm facing the lower-right and the fingers pointing to the upper-right. Both arms thus cross in front of the chest with the left forearm thwartwise upon the right upper-arm. Look in the direction of the right hand.

(538)

Shift your weight slightly rightward and bend both legs to squat yourself down a little more. Meanwhile, both arms joining forces to cross and overlap in front of the chest, with the elbows bent, the palms changed into fists and the centres of the fists facing downward.

(539 - 540)

As you turn your torso promptly and slightly to the right with the hips lowered to form a horse-riding stance, both arms swing to the sides so that the elbows butt explosively backward and a little downward. Keep both elbows bent as slightly as possible with the fists not departing from the chest. Concentrate the force on the tips of the elbows. Look horizontally to the right.

Form 49
Wrapping Firecrackers

(541 - 543)

As you turn your torso slightly to the left and shift your weight completely onto the left leg with the knee straightened, raise the right leg with the knee bent. At the same time, extend the right arm

to the right and rotate it inward. The right fist then sings downward and leftward to the front of the left hip with the centre of the fist facing the right. The left fist drops to the left side of the waist in the meantime.

(544 - 546)

As the left foot drives the floor to jump into the air, the body turns round about 180 degrees to the

right. The right fist continues to swing leftward, upward, forward, downward, drawing a complete vertical circle until it comes to the lower-front-right of the body. Simultaneously, the left fist follows to swing upward from the left side, then chops forward and downward to the front-left.

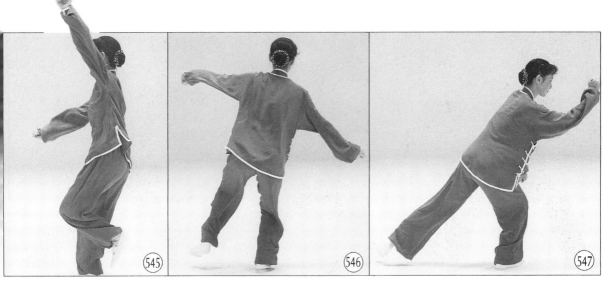

(547 - 549)

As the left foot lands to the left, turn your torso to the right. At the same time, both fists continue to circle. The right fist swings upward and leftward, and the left fist swings downward and rightward. Both arms thus cross in front of the torso with the elbows bent and the left fist out.

(550 - 552)

Turn your torso to the left and shift your weight leftward to form a left-dominated horse-riding stance. Along with the turn of the torso, both fists swing upward and outward explosively, striking to the right and left sides at shoulder level respectively, with the elbows slightly bent and the force concentrated on backs of the fists. Look in the direction of the fist.

Form 50
Dragon on the Ground

(553 - 556)
As you turn your torso to the right and shift your weight toward to the right leg, the left fist swings downward and forward to the front of the abdomen with the eye of the fist on top; while the right

arm moves inward with the elbow bent, until the forearm is held upright in front of the chest with the centre of the fist obliquely facing upward.

(557 - 561)

Turn your torso to the left and shift your weight onto the left leg. Bend the left leg to squat down and stretches the right leg so as to form a right crouch stance. At the same time, the left fist moves upward and leftward to the upper-front of the left shoulder with the elbow slightly bent and the centre of the fist facing the upper-left; while the right fist drops from inside the left arm,

passing before the abdomen, then stretches along the inner side of the right leg to the front, the centre of the fist obliquely facing upward.

Form 51
Step Forward with Seven Stars

(562 - 563)

Turn your torso to the right. Extend the left leg and shift your weight toward the right leg with the knee bent and the toes of the foot turned out, thus forming a right bow stance. At the same

time, the right fist continues to move forward and upward t the shoulder level; while the left fist drops to the side of the left hip; Look in the direction of the right fist.

(564 - 567)

Shift your weight completely onto the right leg. The left foot then takes a step forward with the toes gently resting on the floor to form a left empty stance. At the same time, the right fist moves a little leftward with the forearm rotating outward; while the left fist continues to swing forward and upward with the forearm rotating outward, until it gets close to the outer side of the

right forearm. Both wrists thus cross in front of the chest with the elbows slightly bent, the centres of the fists facing backward. Look in the direction of the fists.

(568 - 571)

With the forearms remaining crossed and rotating inward, both fists revolve round the intersection of the wrists backward, downward, forward

and upward, rolling in front of the chest until the left fist is turned in and the right one out, and the fists changed to palms. Both hands then push slightly forward with the palms facing outward. Look in the direction of the hands. You ought to get the sense of holding the back of your torso firmly backward throughout the push of the hands.

(572 - 574)

Both hands change into fists. With the forearms rotating outward, both fists revolve round the intersection of the fists forward, downward, backward and upward, rolling in front of the chest until the wrists get crossed again with the left one in and the right one out, and the centres of the fists facing backward. Look to the front.

Form 52
Step Back and Mount the Tiger

(575 - 579)

The left foot takes a step to the rear-left. Meanwhile, open both fists and rotate both forearms inward to turn the palms down. As you turn your torso to the left and shift your weight leftward, both hands press down and then separate until they get to the sides above the right and the left knees respectively, with the palms obliquely facing downward.

167

(580 - 583)

Shift your weight onto the left leg and bring the right foot next to the left one with the toes resting on the floor. Keep both knees slightly bent. At the same time, the left hand continues to swing leftward and upward with the arm rotating outward, then moves rightward with the elbow bent, ending with the standing palm in front of the left part of the chest, the wrist at shoulder level, and the hollow of the hand facing the right. Simultaneously, the right circles rightward and upward with the forearm rotating outward, then presses leftward with the elbow bent, until it gets to the front of the abdomen beneath the inner side of the left elbow with the palm facing the left and the fingers obliquely pointing upward. Look in the direction of the left hand.

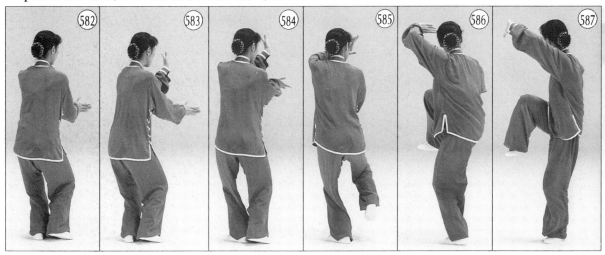

Form 53
Turn Round and Swing Lotus

(584)

Turn your torso slightly to the left and then back to the right. Shift your weight onto the right leg with the heel turned out and the sole of the foot placed fully on the floor. Along with the small twist of the torso, the left hand swings in a small arc counterclockwise with the wrist protruding to the right.

(585 - 588)

Shift your weight completely onto the left leg with the knee slightly bent and the toes of the foot turned out. As you turn round about 180 degrees to the left, the right leg swings leftward and upward with the knee bent. At the same time, the

(588) (589) (590) (591)

left hand continues to swing slightly downward and leftward with the arm rotating inward, passing before the chest, and then moves to the upper-front of the left shoulder with the palm facing outward; while the right hand moves to the side of the right hip with the arm rotating inward to turn the palm down.

(589 - 591)
As you turn your torso further to the left, the right foot lands to the front-right with the toes turned in. Then, shift your weight onto the right leg with the knee slightly bent and raises the left heel with the toes of the foot still on the floor. Along with the turn of the torso, the left hand continues to move to the left side at shoulder level; while the right hand swings to the front-left of the chest,

(592) (593) (594) (595)

with both palms facing downward.

(592 - 595)
Keep your weight completely on the right leg with the knee slightly bent. The left foot swings toward the upper-right and then sweeps round from the right to the left in a fan-shaped arc with the knee naturally straightened. Meanwhile, both hands swing horizontally rightward, slapping

the instep of the left foot successively in front of the chest (the right hand fist, and then the left). Eyes follow the left hand.

169

Form 54
The Head-on Cannon

(596 - 597)

As you turn your torso slightly to the right and bend the right leg to squat yourself down, the left foot lands to the rear-left,. Meanwhile, both hands push to the front-right with the palms facing outward.

(598 - 600)

Turn your torso slightly to the left and shift your weight leftward. At the same time, with the right forearm rotating outward and the left forearm inward, both hands move downward and leftward, changing into fists gradually. The left fist then withdraws to the left side of the waist with

the elbow bent and the centre of the fist facing the torso; while the right fist moves to the front of the abdomen with the elbow bent and the centre of the fist facing upward.

(601 - 602)

Turn your torso promptly to the right and shift your weight toward the right leg with the knee bent. Meanwhile, hold the right forearm thwartwise in front of the chest and the left fist a little beneath and behind the right forearm with eyes of the fists on top. Along with the driving of the left foot and the turn of the torso, both fists together ram to the front-right explosively, with the centre of the right fist facing backward and that of the left one facing the right. Concentrate your strength on the right forearm and the left fist. Look to the front-right.

Form 55
Buddha's Warrior Attendant Pounds with a Pestle and Mortar — Left

(603 - 605)

As you shift your weight further to the right leg, open both your fists. Meanwhile, rotate the right forearm outward and the left one inward. Both hands thus revolve their own wrists clockwise and extend to the front-right at shoulder level with the palm facing outward and the fingers pointing to the right. Then, as you turn your torso to the left and shift your weight toward the left leg, both hands move horizontally round to the left, ending with the left arm at shoulder level and the right one at chest level.

(606 - 611)

As you turn your torso to the right and shift your weight onto the right leg with the knee bent, the left foot takes a step forward with the toes resting on the floor to form a left empty stance. At the same time, the left hand continues to swing downward and forward with the arm rotating outward, until it comes to the front of the abdomen with the palm facing the upper-front and the fingers pointing to the lower-front; while the right hand swings downward and forward with the forearm rotating inward, then upward with the forearm rotating outward, and finally comes back with the elbow bent and the forearm rotating onward, thus drawing a vertical circle until it lies thwartwise upon the left forearm, the palm facing downward. Look in the direction of the left hand.

171

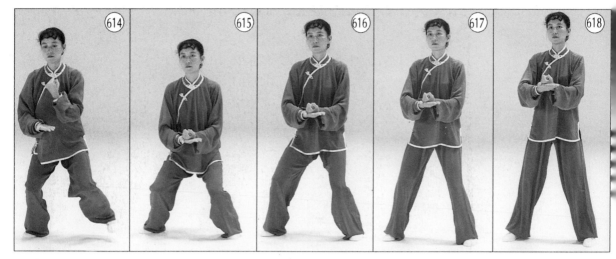

(612 - 613)
Raise the left leg with the knee bent. At the same time, the right hand drops to the front of the abdomen with the palm turned up; while the left hand changes into a fist and rises to nose level with the centre of the fist facing backward.

(614 - 615)
As the left foot forcibly stamps on the floor about 20 cm beside the right one, the left fist smashes down into the right palm with the centre of the fist facing upward.

Form 56
Closing Form

(616 - 619)
Place your weight evenly on both legs. As you

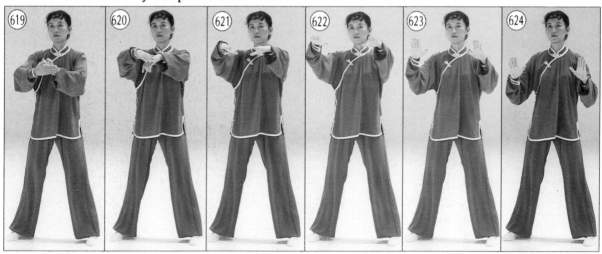

gradually extend the legs, hold both hands up to the front of the chest with the left fist changing back to a palm and both palms facing upward. Look horizontally forward.

(620 - 626)
Rotate both arms inward to turn the palms down, and separate the hands until they are about a shoulder-width apart from each other. Both hands

then fall slowly to the sides of the thighs.

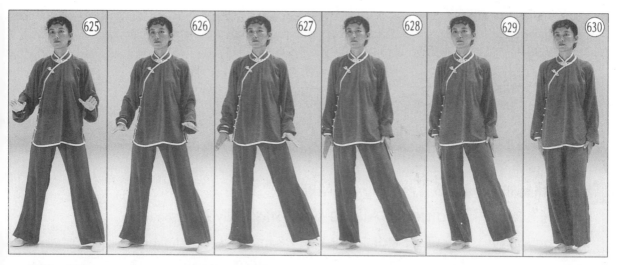

(627 - 635)

Shift your weight onto the right leg and bring the left foot next to the right one. Then, place the weight evenly on both legs with the feet together so as to stand erect. Look horizontally forward.

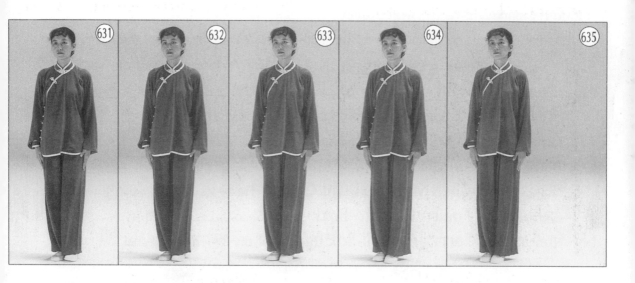

(The End)

Martial Arts Book List